The Desert Mothers

The Desert Mothers

Spiritual Practices from the Women of the Wilderness

Mary C. Earle

MOREHOUSE PUBLISHING

Harrisburg – New York

Unless otherwise noted, the Scripture quotations contained herein are from the New Revised Standard Version Bible, copyright © 1989 by the Division of Christian Education of the National Council of Churches of Christ in the U.S.A. Used by permis-sion. All rights reserved.

Morehouse Publishing, P.O. Box 1321, Harrisburg, PA 17105

Morehouse Publishing, 445 Fifth Avenue, New York, NY 10016

Morehouse Publishing is an imprint of Church Publishing Incorporated.

Cover art courtesy of Corbis

Cover design by Laurie Klein Westhafer

Library of Congress Cataloging-in-Publication Data

Earle, Mary C.
    The Desert Mothers : spiritual practices from the women of the wilderness / Mary C. Earle.
        p. cm.
    ISBN 978-0-8192-2156-8 (pbk.)
    1. Monastic and religious life of women—History—Early church, ca. 30-600. 2. Women in Christianity—History—Early church, ca. 30-600. 3. Meditations. 4. Spiritual exer-cises. 5. Prayer—Christianity. I. Title.
BR195.M65E27 2007
255'.9009015—dc22

                                    2006035215

Printed in the United States of America

10 11 12   10 9 8 7 6 5 4 3

For all the ammas, known and unknown

"You formed us in your own image,
giving the whole world into our care."

–*Eucharistic Prayer D, The Book of Common Prayer*

Contents

Acknowledgments

I am grateful to the staff at Morehouse, who invited me to write this book, and whose confidence in my ability to do so exceeded my own. Nancy Fitzgerald, my editor, has given me solid support, good guidance, and the confidence I needed to finish. Ryan Masteller and the graphics team have provided an evocative cover design and dealt graciously with my questions. Cynthia Shattuck's careful editing brought forth the final version of the manuscript.

This book would not have seen the light of day without the gift of two weeks as a Visiting Fellow at the Episcopal Theological Seminary of the Southwest. That fellowship afforded me the space and time necessary to begin the project. Charles Cook, Cynthia Kittredge, Nance Busbey, Nancy Bose, Rob Cogswell, and Mikail McIntosh-Doty were among the good friends and guides who made those two weeks in the spring of 2005 so fruitful.

The students who participated in my Desert and Celtic Spirituality class at the Seminary of the Southwest in the fall of 2005 shaped and informed this text more than they know. I thank them for their wisdom, insight, and common sense.

My colleagues at The Workshop in San Antonio, Jane Patterson and John Lewis, have been unflagging in their confidence that I could finish this project, despite the travails of the last year.

My husband Doug has helped me by reading and by listening, by encouragement and theological discussion, proving that he has the patience of a desert abba.

CHAPTER 1

Introduction

Where Are the Mothers?

In the late 1980s, as I began life as an Episcopal priest, I kept wondering where all the women were. We had learned of church fathers, desert fathers, and male apostles, bishops, and martyrs. That was all well and good, as far as it went. Common sense told me that there had to be many untold stories of women who had lived this Christian faith. I had an intuitive conviction that women had played a far larger role than the scholarship of the time was revealing. I would walk around asking out loud, "Where are my mothers?" "Where are my sisters?" "Where are all of those women without whom there would be no faith, no church, no tradition?"

Thanks to women scholars of the last generation, we are discovering that the women were there all along. We are discovering, often through painstaking, detailed examination of primary texts (scraps of papyrus, fragments of vellum, hints and allusions in texts written by men), that women played an essential role in the early years of the Christian faith. In those first centuries, before the church was marked by the institutional division between East and West, women were functioning in a variety of roles. They were seeking to live out the faith in Christ crucified, resurrected, and living in ways that were authentic and true to the gospel. They were spiritual guides. They were teachers. They were leaders of their monastic communities. And some of them, as Christianity became an official religion of the Roman Empire, became what are known as the "desert mothers" or ammas. The ammas, or spiritual mothers, were women who offered wise counsel to others and who, through that counsel, became "lovers of souls."

These were women who left their established roles and sought to live both in communities and as hermits in the deserts of what are now Egypt, Israel, and Syria. Others established communities in the area that is now Turkey. The desert mothers were many, and they were from a variety of different backgrounds. They sought to embody the Christian faith in simple, straightforward fashion, daily living out the Great Commandment: "You shall love the Lord your God with all your heart, and with all your soul, and with all your strength, and with all your mind; and your neighbor as yourself" (Luke 10:27; Deuteronomy 6:5; Leviticus 19:18).

As I have learned more about these desert mothers, as well as about the many men who lived comparable lives in the arid wilderness, I have discovered the truth of an observation made by scholar Roberta Bondi: "I have found in them a fleshing out of what Christian love is: God's for all of us, ours for each other, God's world, and God."[1] The sayings and the stories that come from these desert sages speak to us in straightforward fashion about *living* the Great Commandment, not just talking about it. These ammas and abbas (the desert fathers) are down-to-earth, blunt, and savvy about what is needed to mend the ragged fabric of human community. They help us become more open with one another, with God, and with ourselves. They name what needs to be named. And they never forget that love of God, love of neighbor, and love of self are patiently knit together by daily practice.

Historical Background

Throughout the pages of this book, we will be praying with the desert mothers. The term "desert mother" may be completely new to you and may sound odd at first. These are women who lived during a particular moment in church history—a time during the fourth century when Christianity had been sanctioned by the Roman Empire and active persecutions had stopped. The desert mothers lived long ago and, in one sense, in a galaxy far, far away. Their cultural and social settings were so very different from our own that in some ways it is hard for us to imagine their daily lives. The church as we know it did not exist. The Bible as we know it was just being formed. As always, different languages and cultures produced varieties of expressions of the Christian faith. Regional differences were appearing, despite all official attempts to create a unified practice and worship.

Even before the time of the desert mothers, women's lives were more varied than we previously understood.[2] Though men were primarily (though not uniformly) the public leaders of both religious and political institutions, women of means sometimes managed their own land and resources. Women of the upper class were literate, and some Christian women were schooled in Latin and Greek so that they might study the scriptures. The home remained the primary sphere of women's lives, yet within the boundaries of the home, women exercised authority. As has often been the case throughout women's history, particular women found ways to live within the accepted structures of their societies and yet also to be true to themselves and to Christ. Others, pioneers in the faith, created new expressions of daily practice of faith, hope, and love.

We know from the New Testament that house churches were often led by women and, as often as not, one woman's conversion would lead to the conversion of her whole household. Saint Paul gives us the names of women who were his coworkers for the gospel. In Romans 16:7, Paul names Junia as an apostle, one sent by the resurrected Christ to proclaim the gospel. Phoebe, a deacon, was sent to the Romans (Romans 16:1). Paul greets nine different women at the close of this letter, clearly indicating their prominence in the very earliest years of the formation of the Christian community.

As the Christian faith began to spread in the second and third centuries, even in the face of a hostile government and the cult of the Roman emperor, women offered their lives as martyrs and refused to recant in the face of torture and death. Their stories form essential threads in the early Christian narratives—women were the equals of men when it came to standing firm and refusing to bow down to the image of the emperor. Blandina, a slave, was martyred in 177 during a persecution of Christians in Lyon and Vienne in Gaul (now France). Perpetua was executed with Felicity and four men in Carthage in 203. They were equals and yet also different, because women had different roles and spheres of influence. Consequently, their choices were shaped and honed by different pressures and assumptions within the social context of their times.

After this period of martyrdom, when the Emperor Constantine made Christianity a legal religion in the Roman Empire, the era of the desert mothers and fathers began. During the fourth century, many faithful Christians began to be distressed by the church's growing alliance with the state. A kind of restlessness began to grow, a desire to live out the faith in a way that somehow would imitate the faithfulness of the martyrs. Yet how was one to be a martyr when there was no more reason for martyrdom? How was a woman to give up her life for Christ when death was no longer the primary way to witness to Christ? What might a dedicated life look like within the new circumstances of Christianity becoming the state religion? Why would a woman go to the desert? Why would she leave behind everything she had known and go to a place full of silence and scarcity? What would motivate a person to shed a life—perhaps a good life—and move to a completely different setting?

As we will see in the following pages, many women began to create and shape lives in the deserts of Egypt and the Holy Land. As ammas (literally, "mothers," but also implying wise guidance and care of souls), women left the urban environments of Alexandria and other cities. These ammas actively chose to leave the known and established. Some became hermits. Some founded communities of women. Their focus was the love of God embodied in daily life, encompassing every person and all of human behavior. Their intention was formed by regular, habitual practice of silence, solitude, and stillness. At the same time, those practices were balanced by companionship with other seekers, generous hospitality, and unexpected charity and forbearance—these women refused to judge their neighbors.

The lives of these desert mothers, while often seeming strange and completely at odds with the lives of women today, happily challenge and subvert many of the cultural norms that impede women's spiritual growth. They offer the comfort that discomforts. The example of their lives, when reflected upon, leads us to ask questions of ourselves as women and of our larger culture. The sayings they have left us, though far fewer than the recorded sayings of the desert fathers, nevertheless direct our gaze away from surface reality. We have collections of sayings from three ammas, Sarah, Syncletica, and Theodora. We have mention of a woman named Amma Matrona. While these four names may lead us to believe there were few women in this movement, a contemporary historian tells us that there were twice as many women as men living in the desert.[3] These figures are not to be understood as census data; they point to the fact that women were more numerous than men in this way of desert spirituality, and that the practice of the desert way attracted many women as a genuine expression of Christian life.

An Invitation and an Introduction

This book is not intended to be an academic text or a history of the desert mothers. In fact, it is not a scholarly text at all, though I am very much indebted to scholars such as Roberta Bondi[4] and Mary Forman, O.S.B.,[5] whose work has made mine easier. I hope that this book will be primarily an introduction and an invitation—an introduction to encounter some of our foremothers in the Christian faith, and an invitation to practice their way of living that faith in our daily lives. Each chapter will include a saying from one of the desert mothers, some reflection and anecdotal material, and suggestions for incorporating various practices into your way of living and praying as an heir of the desert mothers' wisdom.

We will be praying with these desert mothers, and so we will be discovering aspects of their wisdom along with our own. We will be entering into that mutual vulnerability that comes with praying together, that delicately tender space when the gentle action of God's Spirit allows us to reveal our hearts to one another and to God. To pray with these women will mean that we have to come to terms with our own assumptions—about ourselves, about them, about the faith, about the living God. To pray with the desert mothers is to enter into their space, to risk stepping into the vast emptiness of the desert where the sky glitters with stars brought into being by God. To pray with the desert mothers entails coming to terms with our hungers and thirsts, our cravings in the wilderness, our unspoken, wild yearnings for community and for God's presence.

It is a risky business, praying with the desert mothers. Their example challenges our ways of understanding the faith. Their radical departure from the socially acceptable ways of being Christian gives women today a sense of freedom within the practice of faith—a sense of freedom that may be frightening in and of itself. These women chose to respond to God's call to a different life, and they chose in a variety of ways. Their very choosing flies in the face of centuries of mindless interpretation of the story of Eve—that foremother whose taste of the apple has been interpreted again and again to prove that women's wills are maliciously inclined and that any choice women make cannot be well made. Wrong, say the desert mothers. With our feet and our bodies, we choose Christ. With our lives and our wisdom, we choose a creation made in the image of God. With our humility and our obedience, we choose not to judge one another. With our stillness and our silence, we listen for the Voice that speaks every particle of creation into being.

Praying with the desert women takes us back to the basics. They will remind us of the virtues of simplicity and stillness, of silence and of solitude. They will call us to balance and moderation—something western society has all but forgotten. In stark contrast to the continuous indulgence of gluttony that is our cultural norm, the desert mothers remind us of the virtues of fasting—from food, from frenetic activity, from anger, from hurtful speech, from arrogant and mean-spirited behavior. In short, praying with the desert mothers calls us to be open to conversion, to that deep transformation that can only be accomplished by the activity of the living God moving and dwelling within us, working silently, surely, secretly to make us new. They remind us to trust in a Presence that was there long before we were born and will continue long after we are dead and gone. They pull us out of our illusory concerns and teach us to shift our gaze, to deepen our breath, to stop our moving. Come to the desert if you will, if you choose. Come and pray with these desert mothers, who offer you a word and who already, in Christ, pray for you.

CHAPTER 2

Desert Spirituality

"Salvation is exactly this—the two-fold love of God and of our neighbor."

–Amma Syncletica[6]

Sarah. Theodora. Syncletica. Matrona. These names of the desert ammas are hardly familiar to us. In the culture of Oprah and *Elle*, the desert mothers may seem so remote that their lives can't speak to yours. Yet each of the desert mothers, both those whose names we know and the many whose names are lost to us, offer us examples of women choosing to live as genuinely and as faithfully as possible. In each case, their culture and their families had expectations for what a woman's life should look like. The lives of the desert mothers are remarkable primarily for the ammas' ability to offer their lives back to God. This offering took different forms. Some lived by themselves. Others joined communities of women. Others were the heads of their women's communities. Still others became respected teachers of the Christian path. Some came from privileged and wealthy backgrounds, while others had been prostitutes. Some grew up as Christians. Some came to the desert while still not sure about the life of faith. For each of these women, the life of faith became a weaving together of love of God and love of neighbor, a choosing to live out the Great Commandment.

Each woman's history also included a time of unease with what was expected of her, a moment of recognizing that what the living God might be calling her to be and to do was at variance with the various roles her family and her culture had to offer. When we "recognize" someone or something, we know again ("re" = again; "cognize" = to know). When we recognize ourselves, we remember who we are called to be. We see again that our lives are offered to us as gifts, and that what we do with those lives—how we live every day—is important. By practicing this openness to recognizing both our faults and our deeper call to live authentically in Christ, we learn from the desert mothers. We become more honest with ourselves and with God. We take the time to reflect on our lives. We go back to the basics.

Radical Forgetting and Conversion through Remembering

In this desert tradition, the primordial sin is the sin of forgetting— forgetting that God brings us into being and that each life is a treasure; forgetting that at the end we return to the God who creates us, redeems us, and sanctifies us. When we forget that we are crafted by divine skill, we lose the sense of our own sacredness and we lose the awareness of the sacredness of our neighbor and of all that has been created. The call of the desert is a call to remember the wisdom of the psalmist:

For it was you who formed my inward parts;
You knit me together in my mother's womb.
I praise you, for I am fearfully and wonderfully made.
Wonderful are your works; that I know very well.

(Psalm 139:13–14)

It also tends to be the case that when we lose sight of being "wonderfully made," we fail to see other persons or the creation in that light. The desert tradition took as perennial truth the scriptural description of humanity as being made "in the image and likeness of God" (Genesis 1:26). In the desert, men and women sought to recover the image of God in themselves and in one another. This meant that each person who went to the desert inevitably had to become vulnerable enough to admit her or his own behaviors that covered up or sullied that image. Then, each woman began the lifelong collaborative endeavor of creatively working with God to become the woman she was called to be. This process was a painstaking recovering of identity in Christ.

Because the desert tradition so emphatically proclaims the mercy and graciousness of God, this kind of vulnerability and honesty is truly possible. Each woman's faithfulness in growing in the image and likeness of God benefited not only herself, but also the whole community. As each woman began to know herself as a beloved friend of God, her community was strengthened and made new.

Beyond that, the understanding of the desert elders was that such awareness and practice benefits the whole cosmos. When a woman made the choice to become more truly the person she was called to be in Christ, it was not the first step in a self-help program. The choice to enter the desert was the choice to trust the divine Presence to restore the essential beauty and grace of each person, for the life of the whole world. As each woman, each man sought to live as honest and as simple a life as possible, the immediate community benefited, and—from a faith perspective—that practice of taking the risk of being made new allowed creative possibility to indwell the whole world. Life in the desert was life offered back to the God from whom it came. The whole universe was being made new, bit by bit, person by person, life by life.

Learning to Not Judge

One of the most startling aspects of the spirituality of these desert mothers was their insistence on not judging the actions of others. In our society, where the judging of others is constantly encouraged and practiced, this refusal to judge seems almost absurd. The desert mothers based their insistent refusal to judge their neighbors on the merciful love of God revealed in Jesus. They perceived that God's mercy encompasses all human failure and that if God is willing to be merciful, then so should we. In part, the ammas were able to come to this conclusion because, in becoming aware of their lives as gifts from God, they were also aware of being creatures. There is no such thing as a self-made desert mother. In fact, that term, "self-made," would have confounded the ammas. Their perspective was first to notice the grace, mercy, and love of God that has brought everything that exists into being. To begin to love God and love our neighbor, we need to begin with recognizing that we did not make either—neither God nor neighbor. For that matter, we did not make ourselves.

Being in a desert or in a wilderness helps us to recognize that we are small, mortal creatures. Some years ago I made a retreat at Christ in the Desert, a Benedictine monastery near Abiquiqui, New Mexico, after I had felt the call to silence and to the wilderness. I well remember the drive on a dirt road above the Chama River, which flowed strongly and swiftly, swelled with snowmelt. I kept thinking that if I were to drive accidentally into the river, no one would know where I had gone. My first awareness, before I even reached the guesthouse door, was that my life could end at any moment. I felt very insignificant beneath the red and ochre cliffs and the vast blue sky. By the time I had actually entered my room, unpacked, and begun to fully arrive in that holy space, I realized that I was being invited to reflect on the littleness of my life, the fragility of it, and the beauty of it as well. I'd had a scare with cancer, and I'd been through some rough patches with close relationships. I thought I'd gone away to focus on those issues. However, while they were *part* of my prayer and reflection, those issues became secondary to my recognizing anew that, in some indefinable way, through the journey itself, through walks in the wilderness, through the uncontrolled force of the swollen river, through the thousands of stars I could see without city light, the living God was beckoning me to recognize that I was a tiny part of an interdependent, stunningly wild, and undiscovered universe. During my first retreat at Christ in the Desert, I discovered a kind of medicine that the desert ammas knew—a medicine for the cure of souls, a medicine that helped me to see my life from a completely different perspective and to recognize the beginnings of a new life path.

One evening after vespers, several women were sitting together outside the monastery chapel. I went to sit with them. Though silence was the rule, we decided to speak to one another of our prayers and our aches, our journeys to the desert and our hopes. Later, I realized that each of us, in her own way, was struggling to love God, neighbor, and herself. Having spent so many days in silence, we were delivered from the presumption of speaking out of our old scripts. Our conversation was honest, funny, and real. Each woman was finding the desert time to be healing in and of itself. And each woman was recognizing that the letting go of old identities, old ways of seeing God, old behaviors was both a struggle and a release.

As darkness fell, we remarked on the fact that we were on retreat during the Great Fifty Days of Easter. What better time to allow new life to rise within us? What better time to be in the desert and allow the mercy of God to heal us and make us new, to make us more fully alive? Love of God. Love of neighbor. Love of self. Practice. Practice. Practice. The time in the desert allowed me to see God at the center of everything—a kind of holographic presence, the Christ in whom "all things hold together" (Colossians 1:17). Over the years, since that first desert retreat in 1991, I have noticed, as John Chryssavgis remarks, that the desert is not only a place, it is a way.[7] The desert is a way of living, of learning to be fully human, of learning to love. Every day offers us the possibility of remembering and recognizing the presence of God in us, with us, through us, healing us and making us new.

Suggestions for Prayer and Reflection

1. If possible, spend some time either alone or with a friend in a local park or nature preserve. Be wise about where you go, taking personal safety into account. If you have never done this before, you might ask friends for suggestions. Once you have chosen the place and have put yourself in the landscape, allow yourself to notice the natural world around you. Pay attention to flora and the fauna, from tiny to huge. Notice the life that is going on all the time without being managed by human intervention. Make a list the various plants and creatures that you see. As you observe the landscape, be alert also for your own responses. What feelings and thoughts come to you? Who do you find yourself to be when you are not in your native habitat? What questions and insights does this raise?

While you are in this natural environment, pay attention to your senses. Notice what you see, hear, touch, smell, taste (sometimes, for example, you can taste a strong wind). Notice what you become aware of through your senses. Then offer a prayer of thanksgiving for each sense and for the knowing that comes through sensory awareness. Lastly, bless God for the habitat in which you are praying, taking time to observe carefully the various and diverse forms of life that are within your visual and auditory field. You could offer a blessing along these lines: "I bless you for blessing us with the blessing of this place" (see Ephesians 1:3).

2. In his book *Soul Making: The Desert Way of Spirituality*, Alan Jones points out that in the desert we need food, shelter, and hospitality.[8] In your own life, when have you experienced a "desert time," a time when you were experiencing loneliness, fatigue, or despair? How did God's mercy come to you? If you did not experience mercy, what did you experience? Who were your "neighbors"? How was God present to you in and through those neighbors?

3. For this activity, you will need a large sheet of blank paper and crayons, colored markers, or colored pencils. Trace or draw a large circle, representing the earth. Sketch in your continent and the surrounding seas (this does not have to be perfect—the aim is to pray through the practice of drawing). As you sketch in the continents and the seas and then color them, reflect on love of God, love of neighbor, and love of yourself. Using whatever color you wish, make a dot that represents you within this larger circle of life. Add the surrounding atmosphere, sun, moon, stars. When you have completed the drawing, place it where you can see it daily. Let it serve to invite you to pray: "Love of God, love of neighbor, love of myself."

4. Once when I was very ill and in pain in the hospital, a nurse appeared—seemingly out of nowhere—and placed a cool compress on my forehead. That act of mercy allowed me to get through a diagnostic test and to wait for pain medicine. Reflect on moments when you have known mercy, moments when someone has extended themselves unbidden to come to your aid or to offer comfort. Write these in your journal, and give thanks for the person who embodied mercy.

5. When have you extended mercy to another person? When have you withheld judgment, acted kind, initiated relief for

another who might not have had a claim on your life? How did you feel about your actions?

6. When have you been merciful with yourself? When have you forgiven yourself past mistakes and failures? When have you suspended your own self-judgment in deference to the love and mercy of God?

Closing Prayer

God of all mercies, draw me ever deeper into the mercy in which I live and move and have my being. Grant me the courage to have mercy on myself and on my neighbor. Deliver me from judging harshly. Gentle my heart, for your love's sake. Amen.

CHAPTER 3

The Little World of Ourselves

"We carry ourselves wherever we go and we cannot escape temptation by mere flight."

–Amma Matrona[9]

You may be thinking to yourself, "Of course, I could be whoever I am called to be if I pulled up stakes and left. What does desert spirituality offer someone who has to stay put?" Amma Matrona's saying reminds us of a spiritual truth. No matter how far we flee, we always carry who we are with us. The desert mothers left their immediate contexts not to run away, but to encounter themselves and to encounter God.

"What does that mean?" you may be asking. How can it be possible to find ourselves? Perhaps a present-day example will help make this clearer. A friend of mine (whom I will call Nancy) recently said to me, "Now that I'm forty, I wonder about whether I have chosen the life I was supposed to live. Sometimes I feel this gap. Who I want to be doesn't fit with who I am. And I am puzzled by how that happened, puzzled by the way my life got away from me. Where is God in all of that?"

My friend's self-reflection happened after she chose to make a three-day silent retreat. She is a lawyer, married to an engineer, and they have two children. The press of family, work, social commitments, and care of her mother has been stressful. Her community of worship offered the retreat, and she knew she needed to go. She is a fairly gregarious and extroverted woman, so I was surprised by her choice. She saw the brochure for the retreat and knew in her bones that the time had come for quiet.

During those three days, the retreat leader offered several meditations each day, and the participants prayed together. In between those times, they kept silence, refraining from any conversation. When Nancy first arrived, she was a little nervous. After dinner, as the group prayed night prayers, she began to register her own fatigue. She slept a lot the first day and realized with a bit of shock just how deeply tired she was. By the second day, she began to hear her own questions. That afternoon, Nancy spent some time with the retreat leader, trying to catch up with herself and to sort out the various thoughts and feelings that were coming to her attention in the quiet. She felt both relief and some anxiety—not unlike opening a closet door that has been closed for some time and discovering that it definitely needs to be cleaned out. While Nancy did not come up with any answers during the three-day retreat, she started the process of choosing well, of seeking through prayer and guidance to live her life more intentionally, more prayerfully. For Nancy, this was not so much a matter of doing *more*. If anything, it was a matter of taking stock and letting go of some of the busyness. Nancy recognized in her heart of hearts that she was missing the life God had given her to live and that external trappings, while basically good, were not meeting her soul's yearnings.

Nancy has proved to herself that she can do just about anything and everything. She has succeeded in the profession of law. She is smart, efficient, organized. She has good kids. She loves her husband, though they don't get to spend a lot of time together. And she is now wondering if it's time to ask different questions of her life and of God. She wants to listen more deeply for what God may desire for her. She wants to lessen that gap between who she is inside and who she is in the life she lives.

Nancy's quandary, while framed by the social and cultural context of her city in the United States today, has deep universal themes within it. These yearnings, these unbidden tugs toward living an authentic life, come to us when we sometimes least expect them. Sometimes they come when our lives have been shattered by illness or divorce or the death of someone dear to us. Sometimes we're minding our own business and a word or a story opens an inner door that had been locked shut, and we start the process of reflecting, questioning, examining, choosing.

Ultimately, we cannot escape ourselves and we cannot escape God. We do carry ourselves wherever we go, as Amma Matrona remarked. When Nancy went on retreat, she carried with her the microcosm, the little world of her life. On retreat, she did not have to answer her cell phone, check her e-mail, or check with other moms about the carpool schedule. Her clients could not reach her. On one level, she put down her life; on another, she carried it with her. By choosing to step aside and reflect, Nancy allowed herself gently to begin a process of taking time to be still, to be silent, to be in solitude. She began to stop, listen, and move intentionally into the life of loving God, loving herself, loving her neighbor.

Nancy did not run away. After being nudged and encouraged by her pastor and her inner longing, she said "yes" to a desire to begin listening more deeply to her heartfelt yearnings and to find out what was going on within her. Stepping aside from her life for three days allowed her to begin to notice things that her stressful schedule simply would not permit. She realized, for one thing, how deeply tired she was. And she realized that as she watches her mother age and diminish, questions about the meaning and purpose of her own life were beginning to surface and ask for attention. She carried herself into the little desert of the retreat.

The Desert as a Way of Life

The desert mothers lived in a silence and stillness that we can scarcely imagine. By stepping into a landscape that was wilderness, they left behind the noise of the city. The ammas chose to attune their inner hearing to the movement of God's Spirit within their hearts and souls. Their lives were marked by a desire to listen deeply. The silence of the landscape allowed them to hear the silence of God, the silence from which all creation is spoken into being.

The first invitation of the desert mothers to us is to stop and seek the space and time to listen. For some readers, this may take the form of a silent retreat. For others, it may entail sitting on the porch after the kids are in bed instead of listening to television. For others, it may mean not answering e-mail or getting on the Internet for half a day. Still others may discover it by being in the car alone, with no radio or music playing. The wisdom of the desert mothers tells us that this way of life does not require a physical desert. It does require creating regular space and time to be still and to be silent.

As we, like Nancy, step aside from the rush and press of our daily lives, we can actually notice what is unfolding, day to day. We grow in gratitude as we take the time to simply pay attention to what is happening. We follow Amma Matrona into the desert, carrying ourselves, and we recognize God's presence in and through our daily experience.

Suggestions for Silence and Stillness

1. The desert mothers lived in wilderness. They took up residence in little huts or caves and lived very simply. They invite us to step aside from our full and noisy lives and to find opportunities to notice the self that we carry.

Within the structure of your own daily rhythm, find a time simply to sit still for ten to fifteen minutes each day. This could be at any time of the day. If possible, try to sit in the same place each time. As you sit, gently notice your breath. Pay attention to the rhythm of breathing in and out.

As your breathing eases, notice your body. You may become aware of places that are feeling tight or constricted. Begin to gently stretch and move those places.

Return to gently attending to your breath.

Now, notice your surroundings. What do you see? What do you hear? What do you smell?

If you miss a day, do not despair. Everyone misses a day or two or more. Return to the sitting and pay attention to what you see, hear, smell.

If you care to, keep a simple journal about your experience of sitting still. The sitting itself is prayer. The sitting itself is an opportunity to step aside, to notice, to allow the divine Presence to make itself known to you. This is an invitation to rest in God's restorative silence.

While words are not necessary for the practice, if you wish to offer a *short* prayer of thanks, do so. The desert tradition does not encourage lengthy, long-winded prayers. The emphasis is on becoming aware of God's presence that is always with us.

2. Amma Matrona tells us that we carry ourselves wherever we go. If you could carry a small symbol of yourself, what might that be? A short meditation that might help you discover your symbol follows. You may want to record the meditation first, and then use the recording as a meditative guide. This is not necessary; it is simply an alternative to reading to yourself.

Begin as described above. Find a place to sit (doing this in the place you have designated for your daily stillness would be a good choice). Breathe gently. Place your hands on your lap, palms up, and allow your hands to be at rest. Close your eyes. Imagine that in your hands you are holding a box. Notice its weight, its texture. Let your fingers explore how the box feels. This box contains a gift for you, a gift from the God who creates you in this very moment. Within the box is an offering of love. And, because it is a gift, there are no strings attached.

In your imagination, gently open the box. What do you see? What is there waiting for you to discover? Take the gift in your hands and hold it very gently. As you hold it, offer a prayer of thanksgiving. Begin to observe the details of your gift. Then place it gently back in the box. You may return at any time to hold the gift in your hands.

Now gently return to noticing your breath, and allow your awareness to focus on your present surroundings. You could end by praying: "In the name of the living God. Amen." Or you could simply be quiet and still.

Now that you have a symbol of the self that you carry, you may want to explore that gift symbol. If you wish, write about your experience of the meditation. What was the symbol? How did it feel to hold it? What does the symbol suggest to you about God's gift of your self?

You might want to sketch or paint the symbol or recreate the symbol in clay, or create a collage from magazine pictures or construction paper. How you respond to this symbol for the self that you carry may be expressed in a variety of ways. The important thing is to respond in some way so that the symbol may be enlivened and the prayer may deepen.

Closing Prayer

Gracious God, you have created me in your image and likeness, and I will thank you because "I am marvelously made." Grant me a deepening desire to sit still with you, and to begin to know your love for me. Amen.

CHAPTER 4

"Go to Your Cell"

"If you find yourself in a monastery, do not go to another place, for that will harm you a great deal. Just as the bird who abandons the eggs she was sitting on prevents them from hatching, so the monk or nun grows cold and their faith dies when they go from one place to another."

–Amma Syncletica[10]

In the desert communities of the fourth and fifth century, women were encouraged to stay put. Once a woman had found the right place for her, she was not to flit from one monastic community to another. The desert way values going deep, and going deep requires staying put. While on the one hand, these counsels from the desert mothers refer to one's physical shelter, from an inner perspective, Amma Syncletica is counseling us to not run from ourselves. She is encouraging us to stay faithfully with whatever new life is being hatched within us.

In all probability, you are not reading this as a member of a monastic community, so you may be wondering what Amma Syncletica's words have to do with your life and prayer. On the one hand, Syncletica is writing about the vowed life of the Egyptian desert in ancient times. On the other, she is addressing a universal human temptation—to miss our lives by living completely on the surface. After all, our culture encourages competition and ambition, and we are highly mobile. If we are not careful, that mobility can create a kind of rootlessness that will injure us and those with whom we live and move and have our being. This is the kind of rootlessness that is internal, that is caused by our not staying with anything long enough to grow deep roots. Any gardener will tell you that pulling up a plant and moving it repeatedly does not contribute to the health of the plant. The cultural dilemma of mobility often is beyond our control. The spiritual response of finding ways to put roots into the soil of prayer and faith will support us even when our external lives are mobile.

In the desert, men and women were counseled, "Go to your cell and your cell will teach you everything."[11] The cell was often a small, unadorned hut, perhaps a cave hewn from rock. In any event, the cell was a sacred space, a place in which a woman could be with herself and the divine Presence and listen. The cell was a place of divine encounter and of ongoing, daily experience of being immersed in God's presence.

Amma Syncletica's counsel with regard to this uses a tenderly maternal metaphor—that of the mother bird hatching her young. Each woman in Syncletica's community would have been formed by this teaching as it was repeated and handed down. The life of faith looks like a mother bird, sitting on her eggs. For all we know, that mother bird has moments when it seems like nothing is happening. There are moments when real boredom sets in and the temptation to leave the eggs and do something more interesting arises.

Amma Syncletica's metaphor speaks directly to one of the dilemmas of the spiritual life—that of coming to terms with the plain old ordinariness of spiritual practice and the life of prayer, of the whole of life becoming prayer. Instead, we are encouraged not to sit, not to persevere, not to struggle with boredom. We are enticed by a variety of means to leave our "eggs" and simply move continually from one interest to another. The result is that we don't allow ourselves the opportunity to bring forth new life. The "eggs" die because they are not tended. We miss the deeper life of the Spirit because we are constantly moving from one interest to another rather than focusing on one thing.

Our ancient mothers knew that when boredom threatened, it could very well be the outward and visible sign of God's secret, hidden, inner work within the human heart and soul. Consequently, they emphasized staying in the cell, in the little room of daily living, and letting that cell be their teacher.

What does that mean, letting the cell be our teacher? For one thing, it means that there is a blessing in persevering when a practice gets boring. We are overstimulated and overextended, and the consequence of that is stress. Doctors and researchers tell us that stress is not only a mental condition. Stress creates real physical distress and is a causal factor in physical maladies from heart trouble to cancer. Never-ending stress leads our immune systems to malfunction, and that in turn hurts our bodies. It is hard for us to know the innately humane rhythm of life as long as we are harried and hurried. We become strangers to the persons God calls us to be, simply for lack of steadiness.

Staying in the cell, or "sitting on the eggs," means noticing our appetite for overstimulation. The cell teaches us to slow down, to be less of a slave to our impulses, to notice what is right in front of us. The wisdom the desert mothers offer us is that by staying with ourselves, with our inner ups and downs, with our hurts and our fears, we will bring forth the new life that God is creating within us. The cell teaches us to trust in the Presence even when it feels like absolutely nothing is happening. The cell helps us to see that skipping from one activity to another, from one interest to another, from one focus to another results in never putting down roots, never getting to deeper meaning and purpose, never going beyond surface reality.

Sondra and Her Cell

A friend, Sondra, is in her mid-thirties. She is divorced, and she is in a recovery program for persons addicted to alcohol. After a year of participating in the program, Sondra went on a spiritual retreat for alcoholics and, while she was there, found herself wondering just *who* she is, besides being an alcoholic. "Surely there is more to me than that," she told me. "Surely there is a different Sondra, a Sondra I have yet to really meet." She is right, and the desert mothers would agree with her fully. The addiction to alcohol is a distortion, a terrible ruination of her life. Sondra is in the process of waiting, watching, trusting. She is trusting that new life is forming within her, a life that God is bringing forth, a life that needs tending and care.

Sondra began the practice of choosing well when she went to her first meeting of Alcoholics Anonymous. She continued the practice as she found a sponsor, learned more about the program, and sought to be real and honest. Her "nest" (to follow Amma Syncletica's metaphor) is the structure of the Twelve Steps. The steps give her a pattern for the re-creation and renewal of her life.

Sondra has come to a new juncture. She has, for the time being, thoroughly examined her history of addiction. Now she is yearning for the other part of her story—the part that is yet to be told. Sondra is ready to uncover and discover her innate goodness. She is ready to explore creatively just who she might be if she begins to accept that she is of infinite worth, beloved and cherished by God. She experiences moments of frustration and impatience. She is ready for the hard part— the waiting and the patience, the daily need to deal with her impulse to have a glass of wine—to be over, and she knows that it never will be.

Sondra decided to create a "cell." She set aside a chair in her apartment. It sits in a corner, and there is a window on one side. Next to the chair, she placed a table, and on the table she placed her journal, her Bible, and her prayer book. An icon of the Virgin Mary holding the Christ Child hangs on the wall above the chair. Sondra felt that this particular icon helped her remember that, through her ongoing recovery, she was being called to care for her newly emerging self-in-Christ. The "cell" in her apartment is both prayer space and space for sitting and feeling held by God. Sondra's outward cell has given her a way to discover and to embrace the sacred space that has been within her since the moment of her creation. The space dedicated to reflection and prayer, the place where she can gently sit with the life Christ is bringing forth in her, gives her a steadiness and a grounding that she needs.

Another friend, Claire, works as a pharmaceutical representative, a job that requires her to travel several times a month. At least ten nights a month she is on the road, sleeping in hotels. For Claire, it became necessary to find ways to make the hotel rooms little cells so that she would be more inclined to practice her fifteen minutes of sitting and listening, reflecting and praying. When Claire packs her bag for her trips, she includes a candle, a Bible, her journal, a photo of her children, and a small cross on a stand. When she unpacks, she clears a space and sets up these items as reminders that the true cell is the one that God, through Christ and the Holy Spirit, creates within us.

Suggestions for Creating a Cell

1. The first step in creating a cell (or a "nest," to use Amma Syncletica's metaphor) in your living space is prayerfully to walk from room to room and notice if a particular spot seems to be right. You may know that you need a window. Or you'll know that you want an enclosed space. (I have a friend who set up her prayer cell in a closet.) Keep an open mind and heart as you walk through the place where you live.

You may wonder if such a thing is possible, given the number of people who live in your house or apartment. One woman I know designated a stair on the staircase as her cell. She would go to the same stair to sit every day, carrying her grandmother's shawl and a journal with her.

You also may discover that the place you are called to is not the first place that you choose. If, after trying it out for a few days, the place does not fit, feel free to try a different space. Listen to your body—are you able to be relaxed and also gently attentive? If you are choosing a chair, does it support your spine?

2. Once you have chosen the space for your cell, you may want to adorn it so that it is set apart for prayer, listening, sitting still, and reflection. You may want the area of your cell (which may be a corner of a room) to be simple and plain. Or you may want photographs or icons or other religious symbols on the walls. The point is to create a space that feels like an outward representation of your inner desire for communion with God.

3. You may want to situate a table or a basket in the cell— something to hold a journal, a Bible, a prayer book, a book of devotional readings. Or you may want nothing of the sort. Again, the point is to create a space that is a reflection of your personal prayer and the ways in which God is revealed to you. My own space has some fossils in it, reminders of the creating activity of

God that has gone on long before I came into the world and that will continue after my death.

4. You may want to include space for a companion pet who insists on being part of the prayer (my cat Cuthbert inevitably joins me for morning prayers). You may want to have flowers or a plant in your cell—something green and growing. Your cell may become both a space apart and a space that represents the various aspects of your life. I like to garden, so sometimes herbs from the garden end up in my cell space.

5. Once you have settled on a particular place and have arranged it, begin doing your regular prayer time in that place. If you can do this at the same time every day, it will help you establish a regular habit of showing up for the prayer. In a way, it is almost as if the cell is waiting to greet you (or as if the prayer represented by the cell is waiting for you). The desert mothers knew that the spiritual life is always embodied. Our ongoing life of prayer is shaped by space and time; if you take the time to create a prayer cell and to enter that sacred space regularly, something profound begins to happen in the daily routine. You begin to notice the subtle inner movements that signal new life, and you begin to honor those movements by creating habits that support and nurture the new life. Learning to love God, neighbor, and self with all our heart and mind and strength is learned by daily, ordinary, sometimes boring regularity. The eggs in the nest are not hatched overnight. It takes time and patience. It takes trust. Over a period of days, weeks, months, you will realize that your main responsibility is to show up—to go to the cell and to be still. And let the cell teach you everything.

6. If you travel regularly, you may want to begin to pack a few items that allow you to have a cell in rooms on the road. You don't need to have a whole suitcase full of crosses and icons. One well-chosen item could be all that you need. The point is to

carry something with you that helps remind you to take time for silence and stillness, even in a Holiday Inn.

Closing Prayer

Gentle and loving God, I desire to be still and know that you are with me and within me. Grant me the wisdom to allow my soul to be quiet and confident, trusting that you are doing better things for me than I can ask or imagine. Amen.

CHAPTER 5

Learning the Art of Discernment

"We must direct our souls with discernment."

–Amma Syncletica [12]

A beautiful and educated woman, Amma Syncletica began her life in Alexandria, in Egypt, in the fourth century.[13] She was one of four children; her brothers died and her sister was blind. In other words, despite her privilege, she was acquainted with loss and sorrow. When her parents died, Syncletica gave all of the family wealth away, cut off her hair, and set out for the desert with her blind sister.

They had been reared in Alexandria as Christians, so Syncletica and her sister knew the basics of faith and practice. They had knowledge of scripture. They had been part of a worshipping community. In the desert, Syncletica and her sister made a radical departure from the life that they had known. As they divested themselves of the material goods of their family, in a way, they died to their old life. Clearly, it was not necessarily a bad life. Her parents were, as far as we know, respected in the community. No doubt she and her sister could have stayed in Alexandria and continued to live in the pattern established by their family. Instead, Syncletica and her sister left their home and chose to enter the desert, new and strange territory.

Syncletica's life points to the life of the heart, the soul. She knew that what matters most is to avoid a life crowded with so many cares and concerns that the capacity to choose well is forgotten or weakened.

This is true for us today. Even as we are raising children, working at our jobs, dealing with laundry, meals, grocery shopping, we can remain grounded in truth and love. Each of us is created to embody the life of faith and hope and love. With patience and care, with perseverance and practice, we may discover within ourselves the pearl of great price and, because of that discovery, be able to live with new intention even though the external realities may not have changed that much.

As Amma Syncletica points out, we begin with discernment.

What Is Discernment?

When Syncletica and her sister entered the desert, their journey had begun long before, when the sisters decided that they were called to a life of simplicity. When they began to sense the inner pull toward being unencumbered with goods and possessions, no doubt they began to pray. Their prayer then took the shape of specific actions—the giving away of material possessions and the move toward a different life.

As they prayed and before they acted, Syncletica and her sister went through a process of discernment. They reflected on the choices before them, prayerfully weighing the merits of each choice and then taking the risk of making a decision that they felt was appropriate to their desire to live faithfully. After the decision was made, they made the journey to the desert.

Every day of our lives we are faced with a variety of choices. Every day we chart our paths, both by making choices and by the way we respond to circumstances beyond our control. The hard part comes when we need to make a choice that will affect our lives and the lives of others—our families, our friends, or perhaps those with whom we work. If we have not been taking care on a daily basis to practice paying attention to our lives and to God's presence in our lives, we may be stumped when an important choice is before us.

To choose well, first we have to slow down enough to recognize that there are choices to be made, and then reflect on the various options. When Amma Syncletica offers the counsel that we need to direct our souls with discernment, she is inviting us to live mindfully. She is telling us to slow down enough to be aware of all that occurs within the course of our day. Following the teaching of Jesus, Syncletica is telling us to grow "eyes to see and ears to hear" (Mark 4:9, 4:23; Luke 14:35, 24:31). In the Mark's gospel, Jesus says, "Pay attention to what you hear" (4:24). Likewise, Syncletica is inviting us to notice the choices that come our way and to bring prayerful intentionality to each choice. In the words of educator Parker Palmer, Syncletica is inviting us to "listen to our lives."[14]

Beginning to pay attention to your life, beginning to listen and to see what is unfolding each day in the present, may be a new experience for you. Our culture forms us to be future oriented, which in and of itself is not all bad. However, when orientation toward the future (and a hurried, competitive future at that) is all that we know, we discover a terrible and insidious drying up of life, of the vitality that we are meant to savor and to enjoy, regardless of material circumstance. We miss the delight of simply being alive. Only when we begin a regular practice of discernment do we allow ourselves both the time and space to taste and see our lives, to let the hints and intimations of the life of God capture our attention. We begin to be less driven to seize control. We begin to recognize that there is much in life that we cannot manage, cannot direct, cannot solve. And that realization brings its own kind of freedom. We begin to practice being still, paying attention, listening, and seeing.

In her book *Hearing with the Heart*, Debra Farrington explains,

> *To discern* means more than to understand or to make a decision. *Discern* comes from the Latin *discernere*; *dis* means apart, and *cernere* means to separate. Thus, from all of the choices before us, we "separate apart" those that seem uniquely suited to us. We do that when making a decision as well, but discernment, at least in Christian spirituality, implies that we take God's will for us into account rather than simply our own desires.[15]

Furthermore, the desert mothers would have us understand that God calls us *to live* with discernment. In other words, discernment is an essential aspect of the life of faith, part of the ongoing conversation in prayer with the God who desires for us better things than "we can ask or imagine" (Ephesians 3:20). When we live by practicing discernment, we begin to recognize God's presence and God's love in its many different disguises.

Amma Syncletica would never have expected us to discern well without the help of another. In the next chapter, we will look at the desert mothers' practice of spiritual guidance. For the moment, I hope that you will remember this: the desert mothers knew that the process of discernment never ends. As we stop, listen, wait, and begin to sort through possibilities, we are allowing ourselves to be carried more and more by currents of divine love. Our thrashing about in the waters of life may continue, yet we will also know times of being borne along. We will notice when help and guidance is offered. We will begin to catch ourselves before we act in a way that hurts others or ourselves. Gradually, we will be less inclined to do everything under the illusion of being completely in control and knowing everything there is to know. We will have made those first steps toward the desert way—those first steps that allow God to be at the center of a sacred and living universe brought forth in love, a universe in which each of us is a small and participating part.

There may be moments along the way when an obvious but difficult choice requires much reflection and prayer and guidance. It is also true that, on a daily basis, little decisions and small actions form our souls. We create habits when we make those daily choices. If we choose to act impulsively, without due reflection, we may discover that we have become someone we never intended to be.

While it may come as a surprise that discernment is so essential, Christian spirituality has long maintained that it is necessary for living the faith, not just talking about it. In the prayer book of the Episcopal Church, we find these words in the General Thanksgiving at the end of Morning and Evening Prayer:

> And, we pray, give such an awareness of your mercies,
> that with truly thankful hearts we may show forth your praise,
> not only with our lips, but in our lives,
> by giving up our selves to your service,
> and by walking before you
> in holiness and righteousness all our days.[16]

When this prayer is offered twice a day in a regular rhythm of prayer, the words begin to affect our perceptions and our way of living. The prayer shapes our discernment as we ask for an awareness of God's mercies. Such awareness leads us out of the illusion of thinking that we have made ourselves, and it can startle us into seeing the whole world as God's gift. When we choose to live with discernment, we are no longer at the center of the universe, God is. To put it in plain language, everything is reframed. The frame becomes that of the infinite and merciful living Presence, rather than the much smaller circumference of our own egos.

Graciela is the mother of an eighteen-month-old girl. While Graciela is deeply grateful for the life of this child, she is also missing her work as a nurse. She and her husband are beginning to talk about whether Graciela could go back to work. She has begun her discernment by noticing what she would miss if she returned to her work at the hospital, and imagining how her life would change. She has also begun to write down what she misses about working. At present, she is reflecting on different possibilities—whether to work full time or part time, whether to wait until the baby is two years old, whether to use this time to pursue a certification that would enhance her employment choices in the future.

As Graciela begins to reflect on all the different ways that her life has changed since the baby's birth, she is also recognizing that her desires have changed in some ways. Before she makes a decision, she is taking the time to notice, to pray, to talk to a wise older friend who is also a nurse. In the next several months or so, Graciela will come to a decision, a decision that has been made with care, with awareness, with guidance, and with love of God, love of neighbor, and love of self.

The Role of Silence in the Process of Discernment

When we practice being still and silent in our cells, something begins to happen. We hear all of our inner chatter. And, after a while, we also hear the subtle (and sometimes not so subtle) nudging of the Holy Spirit. Discernment is made possible and supported by regular times of silence. As one author stated, "Silence is *a way of waiting, a way of watching, and a way of listening* to what is going on within and around us. It is a way of interiority, of stopping and then of exploring the cellars of the heart and the center of life."[17] Just as it would be difficult to read this text if there were no spaces between the words, so living without taking time for silence makes our lives a jumbled and garbled text. When we have no time for quiet reflection, we truly miss our lives.

Taking time for silence allows for gentle reconfiguration in a culture that is saturated with noise of every kind. As I write, I can hear cars passing by and airplanes overhead. The phone rings occasionally. My computer makes whirring noises. We cannot go out to buy groceries or to eat in a restaurant without hearing a lot of noise. Deliberately doing without noise allows the body, the heart, and the mind to rest. In the resting, we can discover what is asking for our attention. We can tend to the insistent yearnings that may be promptings from God. We can discover the infinite, deep space between the "words" of our lives.

Josie is a working single mother of three children. For her, the opportunity to rest in silence seems unlikely but, as a first step, she has begun to pay attention to the rhythm of her day. Mornings and evenings are full of the immediate press and noise of the children, fixing meals, running errands. She usually takes her lunch to her job, and had been in the habit of eating in the lunch room at the big corporate office building where she works. Josie decided that three days a week she would, weather permitting, eat her lunch in the small courtyard of the building. She has discovered that eating by herself allows her to decompress, to allow herself to breathe, and to return to an inner quiet. She tries to do nothing more than gratefully eat her lunch and spend time resting from activity, resting in God. She told me recently that this practice, a practice that does not add pressure or seem like one more "to do" on a long list of duties, has given her space and time to remember to pray, to remember to breathe, to remember God's presence.

Suggestions for Silence and Discernment

1. Pick one regular activity (such as driving a car, cooking, taking a bath) that you could do in silence for a week. Do that activity in silence, without music, without radio, without conversation. Notice that you are *not adding a new activity*. You are doing something you ordinarily do, but in silence. Pay attention to your own responses—how do you feel in the silence? Do you notice a difference in your body? As you learn to live with

this particular time of silence, what do you notice about your responses to silence? What memories, feelings, thoughts come in the silence? If you are keeping a journal as you engage these practices, note what gifts and struggles come in your silence. Then pray simple, short prayers under the categories of "help!" and "thank you." For example, after writing down what came to your attention in the silence, you might construct prayers such as "Help me to be patient with my family. Help me to remember the hungry. Thank you for my home, my breakfast, my work." The desert encourages prayer that is direct, honest, and vulnerable.

2. The practice of living with discernment invites us to slow down and to reflect. One way to begin incorporating discernment into your life is to practice a prayer of recollection daily. This is a simple way of reviewing the day's events, remembering what happened in a twenty-four-hour period and prayerfully noticing what might have been overlooked. A prayer of recollection allows us to bring eyes to see and ears to hear to the dailiness of our lives. By taking the time to "collect" all of the bits and pieces of our day, we receive what we have been given. We have an opportunity to notice moments when we failed to be kind, to be forgiving, to be generous, to be hospitable. And we notice when we were the recipients of kindness, forgiveness, generosity, hospitality. We allow God to tell us the truth of our day.

• To do a prayer of recollection, first decide what time of day would work for you. I am definitely a morning person, so I do the prayer of recollection as a part of my early quiet time. Others may find that noon or evening is best. The point is to discover the time that is yours, when you are most likely to show up for the prayer.

• Once you have decided on a time, choose a place. Your cell is a likely place, although if you want to do this prayer at noon, you may be away from the cell. Having a regular time and place creates a sense of habit; we are all more likely to actually follow through on a practice of prayer if we can support prayer with regularity.

• Having chosen a time and a place, find a position that is comfortable for your body and begin by gently noticing your breath. Offer a simple prayer to begin: "Gracious God, grant me eyes to see and ears to hear your presence in the day that is past." Then simply start reviewing the previous twenty-four hours, "watching" yourself go through the various times of day. Who was a part of your day? Where did you go? How did you feel physically? What kinds of activities transpired?

• Once you have reviewed the day, pay attention to what resonates with you during this process of recollection. Recently, when I led a group in this practice, a young lawyer remarked, "I realized how busy I am. I knew I was busy, but I did not realize just how bad it had gotten." Another person remarked that she discovered two lovely moments, in completely different places, that otherwise she would have overlooked or forgotten. She sensed that these moments were gifts that she almost failed to receive. Yet another person observed that the prayer allowed him to remember some intercessions that he wished to make for friends. Discernment always begins with this process of separating and noticing, of becoming aware of what is happening. To direct our souls with discernment, we need to choose silence, solitude, and stillness—subversive choices in a culture saturated with noise, overstimulation, and overextension.

• Begin keeping a record of what you notice. You may discover patterns that you need to be aware of—patterns that are life giving (such as a capacity to enjoy and honor friends and family) and patterns that are life sapping (such as a tendency to be overprogrammed or to be critical of others). As you begin to pay attention, to see and to hear the life you are living, you can begin to make small, intentional choices to reshape your life, reflecting God's love for you and your neighbor in a fruitful way.

• Remember that the desert way radically emphasizes not judging one another. If you uncover patterns in yourself that could bring forth a severity toward yourself or another, seek the counsel of spiritual guide as described in the next chapter. The desert elders knew that the love and mercy of God, shown forth fully in Jesus, is the foundational reality of all that exists. They would never encourage the perpetuation of behaviors that hurt and destroy ourselves or one another. They would invite us to seek help, to begin trusting another to guide us toward restoration and renewal through honesty and struggle.

Closing Prayer

Grant me, dear God, the grace and the courage to be still and know that you are God, the wisdom to allow my soul to wait for you in silence, and the love to choose a path of life. Amen.

CHAPTER 6

Spiritual Guidance

Lovers of Souls

"A teacher ought to be a stranger to the desire for domination, vainglory, and pride. A teacher should not be fooled by flattery, nor blinded by gifts, conquered by the stomach, nor dominated by anger. A teacher should be patient, gentle and humble as far as possible; successfully tested and without partisanship, full of concern and a lover of souls."

–Amma Theodora[18]

The desert mothers and fathers understood that at the heart of the Christian path is the call to be in communion with God and with one another. Such communion is possible only when we encounter each other in vulnerable, gentle ways, marked by mutual respect and forbearance. Learning to live in this way requires practice and role models—teachers who, as far as possible, are patient, gentle, and humble.

Amma Theodora recognized that in the walking of this Christian path, we need a particular kind of teacher. We need teachers who do not exalt themselves, teachers who are also companions and sister travelers. We need teachers who are also guides. We need teachers who don't care about approval or power, but rather desire that each person grow gently and surely into the person God desires him or her to be. We need teachers who are also lovers of souls, who are true ammas.

Amma Theodora uses the word "teacher" in a particular way. This kind of teacher was capable of handing on what she had received through the love of God. By her word and her example, she taught others who were seeking to follow Christ. She did not have a classroom or an assignment book; she was more like a master craftswoman teaching her apprentices. The apprentice learns by watching and imitating the way in which the master does the craft. For example, in learning to weave, I had to learn how to prepare the loom by watching my teacher. Dressing or preparing the loom requires the patient placement of warp threads through the heddles (a larger version of putting a thread through the eye of a needle—some three hundred times). I did not learn how to do it in one session. It took practice and, after six years of learning to weave, I still think of myself as a beginner. Over time, the patterns and habits modeled by my teacher have shaped my own craft. As I have learned from my mistakes and have had to rethread the loom, taking out threads that were misplaced and putting them in the correct slots time and again, I have also begun to be able to build on what I have learned. I am sometimes able to create patterns that are of my own design, although formed by basic instruction. Without this basis, my weaving would likely be inclined to unravel. By analogy, the ammas in my life have also served as teachers for practicing the Christian life, tending to detail and observing the patterns, trying to catch mistakes and faults before they disrupt the whole cloth.

In recent years, this kind of spiritual companioning has received a lot of attention. Sometimes known as spiritual direction and sometimes as spiritual friendship, the relationship practiced by the desert mothers was not the result of a program or a certification process. Rather, for them, the most essential characteristic for a spiritual guide was experience in walking the path herself. They had learned firsthand the difficulties of making choices that went against the cultural grain. A spiritual companion had to become acquainted with her own gifts and weaknesses. She herself had been the recipient of kindly guidance by another. She had befriended herself in the process, as she had been befriended by another. She had entrusted herself to the work of the Holy Spirit, making her new and drawing her into community with the whole created order. She had begun the practice of putting the love of God at the center of her whole life.

Those who were ammas were not gurus in the sense of being spiritual experts with a circle of devotees. These women were not seeking to be known for their spiritual expertise. If anything, they were attempting to live faithful lives, as simply and gently as possible. They chose the desert to be hidden with Christ, and to be made new by letting go of what was false in themselves. A woman who became known as an amma, as a guide and a teacher, received that recognition because of the example of her life. What matters in the desert way is the truth and mercy of one's living. Reputation, celebrity, approval, wealth—all of these are of no importance in the desert. What matters most is to live a life marked by kindness and mercy, hospitality and respect.

In writing about Amma Theodora's life, scholar Susanna Elm points out that Theodora, who lived in the late third century, was so respected that even Bishop Theophilus of Alexandria sought her counsel.[19] Theodora was "a true desert 'mother,' a formidable figure, whose Sayings were sought after by many Fathers."[20] Theodora offered the kind of teaching that has a natural attractiveness to it. Her presence and guidance were the fruit of her own practice of silence and stillness, of the ongoing desire to bring love of God, love of neighbor, and love of self into daily life. She knew the value of a teacher who is a lover of souls because she had no doubt experienced the gently transformative nature of such a relationship. She knew that being able to tell the truth of your life to another, without pretense or artifice, will liberate us from our inner prisons.

"Give Me a Word"

In the desert, women sought counsel from one another. And men sought counsel from women, and vice versa. While solitude, silence, and stillness were the basic structures of the life of the desert elders, they also knew that they needed each other. The desert led them to put away defenses and ways of interacting that might have impeded honesty and vulnerability. In the desert, it became radically clear that the way was made by walking together.

In practice, those new to the desert would seek out an amma for counsel. Usually, the seeker would use the formula, "Give me a word."[21] This communication, which we have received in various collections of sayings and stories, would be direct and concrete. The seeker might ask, "What am I to do about my neighbor whose habits are driving me crazy?" The amma would reply in a way that took into account the specific circumstance of the woman who had come for counsel. The amma would focus on what was particular and singular in the seeker's narrative. And, as a consequence, her reply, always informed by prayer and scripture, would be the healing word needed for a particular person, place, and time. Perhaps a seeker would ask, "How do I forgive?" The amma's answer would take into account the seeker's story of being hurt or rejected, and the amma would listen for the concrete details of the action necessitating forgiveness.

For this reason, when we read the sayings and the stories, at first glance they may seem to be a crazy jumble of bits and pieces. The sayings and the stories, when we reflect on them, lead us to see that God is encountered in the details of our lives and relationships. The desert teaches us to begin to notice how the details of our lives reveal our moments of unfaithfulness and of fidelity to the love of God, love of neighbor, love of self.

Going to an amma for counsel also happened within the context of attempting to live out the Great Commandment. Loving God and neighbor and self are possible because we are first loved by the God who speaks us into being. Knowing that foundational and primary love of God often happens through the presence of another person, someone whose life shows us that love. The amma was to be, above all, a "lover of souls." She was called to love as God loves. The amma who was also teacher and guide had the patience, humility, and perseverance to tend to her own issues, to seek a sister in the desert for her own care, to recognize her own need for the mercy and lovingkindness of God. She had the humility not to worry about her self-image and the grace to know she was not God. As we will see in the next chapter, humility was considered the most important character trait in the desert.

Finding a Soul Friend and Teacher of Love

In our day, the mobility, speed, and superficiality of our society all work against discovering a person who could be a teacher and soul friend for you. Friendship, by definition, takes time. It is a process of mutual self-disclosure. Occasionally, we are surprised by a friendship that is marked by trust and joy and truth almost from the first moment. By and large, however, friendship of this nature—friendship built on the love of souls—takes time, patience, perseverance, and care.

I recognize a potential teacher who is a lover of souls when I see someone whose life makes a difference for the good of her or his community. An older woman in our community has served as a teacher for many by the example of her presence. She is a woman who is well respected in the community, and her presence and her generosity of time and treasure have made a difference to several initiatives to improve the lives of impoverished women in my city.

Teachers are also known by their willingness to continue to learn. As we are told in the Wisdom of Solomon, "The beginning of wisdom is the most sincere desire for instruction" (6:17). This kind of teacher always remains teachable—in other words, a kind of gentle humility dwells at the core of his or her presence.

If I truly desire to find someone who can walk with me, coaching me to perceive what I need to know of my own strengths and weaknesses, I will need to be willing to trust another, to invest time in the relationship, and to be as honest as possible. For example, I won't be able to discover a soul friend and teacher if I think I know everything I need to know. For that matter, if I fear I am beyond help, I won't be able to notice a friendship that God is offering me.

In my own struggles with illness, I have been on the lookout for women who also live with chronic illness, whose lives are marked by that quality of love and feistiness that, for me, prove attractive and encouraging. E-mail correspondence has given me a teacher for whom I am immensely grateful. She is a writer, and she has taught me by example, again and again. Her ability to perceive, even from afar, the love of God in and through the events of my life, has been a gift. Her counsel has allowed me to be more at peace with myself, and to be a little more honest.

Suggestions for Reflecting on Finding and Becoming a Lover of Souls

1. A lover of souls becomes so through experience and struggle, through allowing her own sorrows and joys to deepen compassion. While education and formal programs of spiritual formation may enhance the qualities needed, the most important characteristic of this kind of teaching is an ability to love honestly and wisely. When you reflect on those people whom you have known who love honestly and wisely, what qualities of character did they demonstrate?

2. That kind of love, enhanced by the ability to perceive what is needed for a particular person in a particular moment, is a kind of healing presence for others. Ask yourself who has been this kind of presence for you. What were your circumstances at the time? What did your soul need for healing and growing? How was that other person able to help you? How were you able to receive the counsel being offered?

3. Naturally, some of the best teachers are found in classrooms. When you reflect on the teachers who made a difference in your life, what qualities and values did they manifest? How did those teachers influence you? How is your life different because of them? If teachers who made a difference in your life are still alive, write them a note of gratitude.

4. Who are the teachers you have known who were not in classrooms? For some, these may be grandparents or other older relatives. For others, these may be parents of childhood friends or scout leaders. When you reflect on these kinds of teachers in your life—teachers who were mentors and friends—what gifts did they give to you? How have you changed as a result?

5. Reflect on your own abilities to be a lover of souls. Have you had the experience of being sought out by others for counsel and advice? If you have, how have you responded? How have you handled your own feelings about such interactions?

6. Amma Syncletica said, "It is dangerous for anyone to teach who has not first been trained in the practical life. For if someone who owns a ruined house receives guests there, harm is done because of the dilapidation of the dwelling. It is the same in the case of someone who has not first built an interior dwelling: loss is caused to those who come. By words one may convert them to salvation, but by evil behavior, one injures them."[22] Unfortunately, some people have had the experience of being injured by the behavior of a spiritual teacher who has not done his or her inner work. Syncletica understood that the health of the whole community depends upon the health of each of its members. If you have had an injurious experience with a spiritual teacher, you may find it difficult to begin that sort of relationship again. Nevertheless, keeping the hurt bottled up will make things worse instead of better. It is very important to begin to seek healing; if the experience left you unable to trust church authorities, I suggest that you begin with local mental health resources. The ammas would encourage you to remember that you are called to love yourself.

7. Syncletica's caution leads us to reflect on the areas in our lives that need tending, prayer, reflection, healing, and confession. What parts of your history or behavior do you wish to offer for healing and reconciliation? As you have read this text and practiced some of the suggested exercises, you may want to seek spiritual counsel with regard to misdeeds. Begin with your pastor or priest. Ask for time (around an hour or so) to begin the conversation. In that time, you could ask if the priest or pastor has the time to spend with you as a spiritual companion. If not (and many of them are too occupied with the day-to-day responsibilities of their congregations or do not feel called to this ministry), ask for a recommendation.

If you find that you have something you wish to confess to a priest, know that in the Episcopal Church there is a service called Rite of Reconciliation of a Penitent, found in the Book of Common Prayer.[23] As the directions indicate, the confessor is morally bound to never divulge the contents of a confession; "the secrecy of a confession is morally absolute for the confessor."[24]

Closing Prayer

Gracious God, in Jesus you have called us to be your friends. Make me a lover of souls, and grant me the teachers I need for this moment in walking the path of life. Amen.

CHAPTER 7

The Practice of Humility

"Neither asceticism, nor vigils nor any kind of suffering are able to save, only true humility can do that."

–Amma Syncletica[25]

Amma Theodora's sayings emphasize self-discipline and humility, stressing the creative tension between the love and mercy of God and the human responsibility to respond to the gift of that love and mercy. She also emphasized living "in peace with oneself."[26] To live in peace with ourselves, we first need to practice humility in the desert way. Humility, as understood by the ammas, is not humiliation. It is not thinking of ourselves as worthless or without any capacity to offer work and life for the good of the world. The desert elders understood that we are created in love by God and that at the end of our lives we will return to God. In the way of the desert, humility begins when we understand ourselves to be mortal—odd creatures in whom heaven and earth meet. We are inspirited clay, in whom the very breath of God moves. We savor the beginnings of joyous humility when we recognize that we did not bring ourselves into being, nor did we bring the creation into being. We receive fully the gift of being creatures and of being made in the image and likeness of God. We begin to struggle with behaviors that do not honor that image in ourselves or in one another and the world around us. We practice humility when we allow ourselves, as Roberta Bondi observes, to know we will never be above reproach.[27]

Real humility allows us to take ourselves lightly, to be less concerned with heroic endeavors always to be right, to be kind, to be "the good person." When I am walking in the desert way, guided by these ammas, I know that, because I am "on the way," there are bound to be moments when, despite my best efforts, I hurt another. I may speak a word in anger and must ask forgiveness. Or I might forget to call a friend who is lonely. Humility allows me to notice those moments, those sins of omission and commission, and to seek to redress the situation. The desert way does not gloss over our unjust and demeaning actions toward others, our sinful actions and behaviors. The desert way sees the truth of those actions with clarity and precision, yet always perceives them as much smaller than the vast and unfathomable love of God. The seeker who goes to the amma is assured of entering a cell filled with a mercy and love not of the amma's making, for this is the love of God. As a consequence, the practice of confessing what we have done and what we have left undone becomes far less dramatic. It is similar to washing the laundry, turning the garden, or cleaning out the closet. Paying regular attention to our particular tendencies that disrupt the pattern of love helps us to know ourselves. That awareness allows the love of God to be more and more the central focus of our lives. Humility encourages us to be frank about our shortcomings and failures and to desire transformation.

When we are short on humility, we tend either to ignore our own shortcomings (because to admit them would be to admit that we are human) or to wallow in them. The desert way, which ultimately is downright pragmatic, tells us to "pick yourself up, dust yourself off, and start all over again." I am not intending to be flippant. The desert teachers understood that human life is a process of having the perseverance and the courage to admit our faults, to celebrate our blessings, and to be honest about when we need to stop and then start over, while allowing our teacher, our amma, to remind us of the love of God that will not let us go.

To return to the analogy of learning to weave, an apprentice weaver has moments when she has to take the yarn off the loom and begin all over again. I well remember when my teacher would come to my side, look at the warp threads, and be able to perceive what was hidden from me—missed or crossed threads that would cause trouble with the weaving of the cloth. I would not have seen this by myself because I did not have the experience or the practiced vision. I had to relearn the truth from the Wisdom of Solomon: "The beginning of wisdom is the most sincere desire for instruction" (6:17). Seeking an amma, a teacher, a guide, is possible when we desire instruction, when we have the humility to know that we are ready to seek help and companionship. The apprentice who wishes to learn will have the humility to start over rather than continuing to press ahead, thereby making a cloth that will not hold.

The Practice of Repentance

As we have seen, the sayings of the desert mothers are replete with calls to repent. Following Jesus, they call to us, proclaiming, "Repent, for the kingdom of heaven has come near" (Matthew 4:17). Repentance is not something we like to embrace. If I am to repent, I need to be able to see my life with the eyes of Christ. From the divine perspective, we are creatures but "a little lower than God" (Psalm 8:5) who have thoroughly forgotten that identity. We have allowed ourselves to be reduced to identities such as "I am what I have" or "I am what I do." The desert ammas and abbas, while clear-eyed and rigorously honest about those behaviors that take us away from God, always begin and end with the mercy and creative healing offered by this Christ, in whom "all things hold together" (Colossians 1:17). The human context is always within the divine context; the love of the living Trinity surrounds and upholds us as the ocean surrounds the whales and the porpoises.

Repentance begins with telling the truth about hurts I have caused, sins I have committed, loves I have destroyed. I am able to tell that truth because the mercy and forgiveness of God are always far greater than my sins. Knowing my particular propensities that lead me away from living the Great Commandment allows me to name those propensities and confess them. Then I can be liberated by God's action of forgiveness as I say, "Yes, I did that." And in a society that is thriving on an inability to admit wrongdoing and take responsibility, the ongoing practice of repentance is a lost art.

It is an art because repentance returns us to the beauty of the living God, the beauty of the life of God in Christ, living and pulsing in and through us. Repentance allows us to open ourselves to the love of God that breathes us into being at every moment, despite the fact that we may choose to ignore that. When we begin to be honest, to clean out the inner closets and air the willful acts of putting ourselves first, something truly unexpected happens. We begin to be made new. The desert elders would tell us that our wrongdoings are never the last word. Believing that is to believe we are God; it is to believe that we, rather than God, have the final word on our lives. Humility invites us to repent because we are constantly living in an ocean of divine mercy.

The Passions, or Wounds That Mercy Will Heal

When reflecting on the human propensity to forget our origin in God and behave horribly, the spiritual psychology of the fourth century spoke of "the passions." These "passions" are not what we think of when we normally use the word. They have nothing to do with creative enthusiasm or romantic, sexual love.

Instead, the passions were understood to be wounds in the depths of the soul, wounds that needed the sure anointing of divine mercy and forgiveness. From the perspective of the desert way, each person suffers from the passions in one way or another. The primary characteristic of the passions is that they pervert the vision of love and destroy the workings of love.[28] Habits that are not inclined toward love, the passions afflict us all.

As theologian Frederica Mathewes-Green notes, a passion is a submission to forces that lead us away from God.[29] In other words, the passions subvert the Great Commandment. The passions are patterns in the soul that keep us from walking a "path of life" (Psalm 16:11). Traditional lists of the passions include gluttony, greed, impurity, anger, lust, envy, vainglory, pride.[30] For our purposes, it is not as necessary to catalog each passion as it is to become aware that they exist. Humility allows us to seek the help of another to properly identify and notice the passions at work in our lives. In a way, it's like going to see the doctor when something is awry. If I labor under the illusion that I go to see the doctor to prove that I am well and do not disclose troublesome symptoms, I will never be properly diagnosed. I could become very ill by failing to be honest with the physician. Similarly, if I fail to tell the doctor about

my difficulties in following a prescribed regimen, we cannot collabora-
tively come up with ways to address what needs to be healed.

Similarly, humility allows us first to acknowledge that we need some
help. This first step can often be the hardest. And it is often the case
that stopping, being silent, beginning to watch and to wait allows us to
register discordant and distressing aspects of our own behaviors. My
own experience tells me that it is harder to remain in denial if I am still.
This, as we saw in chapter three, is the wisdom of the cell and of staying
quiet for the sake of new life.

When we are moving at eighty miles an hour through life, we may
not recognize these inner habits and patterns. Of necessity, slowing
down will bring them to our attention. Make no mistake, the desert
way is not a cakewalk. This way recognizes that the spiritual life is a
struggle, a struggle to bring forth new life. It is also without a doubt
a way of mercy and a way of healing, a way of discovering community and solidarity. When you become increasingly aware of your own
inner wounds that create habitual ways of thinking, feeling, and acting
that disrupt and hurt your life and others, you may want to flee this
new awareness. The passions, as the desert ammas understood them,
have us in their grip. Yet Jesus tells us clearly that God is our friend
and our life; we are not without help. God's desire for us is health
and wholeness—for each one of us, and for the whole human family;
indeed, for the whole creation.

We do not often encourage one another in being honest, vulnerable,
and undefended. We cannot deal with the passions in isolation. We
need companions in this journey, and some experienced sister travelers. Often a spiritual guide, a lover of souls, can be of help to us.

Patricia had a long-standing irritation with a friend of hers who
seemed to have an easy life—a good marriage, two healthy children,
some degree of success. Patricia's response to all of this was not joy,
but a kind of incipient jealousy. Patricia was too diplomatic to say out
loud what was going on inside: a kind of ongoing critique of her friend,
a habit of continuously judging her. Although Patricia kept these
thoughts hidden, her inner habit nevertheless affected the relationship.
When Patricia began to seek spiritual guidance and began to look at
her own pattern of reacting to her friend's good fortune, she noticed
this tendency toward envy.

Until Patricia took the time to notice this habit of perceiving and thinking, she was largely unaware of how it contaminated her friendship. When, with some openness and vulnerability, she began to tell her spiritual guide about this inner wound, she took the first steps toward allowing the habit of envy to be transformed.

Mercy, Not Judgment

As John Chrysavvgis has observed, "Our passions indicate not so much that we are doing something wrong, but that we are not in control."[31] Following the teaching of the desert, he points out that the word "passion" is "derived from the Greek word *pathos*, which indicates that we are—as the English word itself also implies—passive rather than active."[32] The habits and patterns known as the passions, when not addressed, act upon us. We discover that we are in their grip and that we cannot seem to find the means to be liberated. We may fall prey to the temptation to ignore the patterns that come from these inner wounds or to excuse them. We may decide that no one could possibly understand. The desert ammas and abbas recognized that these inner wounds required mercy rather than judgment and condemnation. Our human inability to stop these inclinations, which lead to sinful behavior, is both a blessing and a curse. It is a curse because, if we fail to grow in humility, we inevitably become more and more captive to the habits that are destructive of love. Only by growing in humility, by becoming more open and vulnerable with ourselves, with God, and with others, can we receive the mercy that is always offered readily. This inability to heal the passions on our own is also a peculiar blessing, because often when we come to the end of our own resources, we are willing to ask for help. Then we are open to guidance from God and from friends and teachers. The desert ammas understood that our besetting passion, when touched by mercy and grace, could become the precise locus of deepening compassion and capacity for love.

Karen grew up in a family that had been devastated by the Great Depression in the 1930s. Her parents and her grandparents never got over their deep fears that once again there would not be enough to eat, that clothing would be scarce, that employment would disappear overnight. In part because of this familial pattern, Karen discovered that she incessantly wanted more of everything. She was plagued with the passion of gluttony. When she saw new clothes in a catalog, she bought them. If she could not afford them, she felt somehow shortchanged or diminished because she could not have yet another dress. On the surface, this would seem to be a pattern of overbuying and overconsumption. Underneath, however, there is a wound of deep fear that has been passed from one generation to another. The wound is one that was inflicted by the historical circumstance of the Great Depression and by the severe economic distress endured by Karen's grandparents on both sides. Her parents were both profoundly affected by this fear, and so Karen was shaped by the fear from a very early age. Only recently, through patient and gentle attention to her life, has Karen begun to recognize the inner wound that needs healing. As she grows and deepens in love, Karen finds herself particularly drawn to care for those who have lost everything—the victims of Hurricane Katrina. She has started helping an evacuee family that has decided to settle in her city. Her fear of not having enough, which had resulted in a form of gluttony, is healing as she reaches out to those who have lost home, livelihood, and every material possession.

The desert ammas and abbas tell us that the passions are wounds that will heal from the inside out. There is no quick fix for these passions, these patterns that are destructive of love. Instead, we are offered a gracious way *through* the wounds, through the loving practice of seeking to be less identified with the passions and more identified with the living Christ who dwells within us, even when we are least capable of honoring that indwelling.

Suggestions for Practicing Humility

1. The world "humility" comes from the Latin *humus*, which means "earth." One of the ways in which we learn about humility is by being in contact with soil by planting seeds. As we cultivate plants, we cultivate humility. Experience in planting and gardening quickly teaches us that we are not in control, though we do participate with God in the growing of green things. Your "garden" could simply be a flowerpot with soil and some parsley seeds. Or it could be a small plot in your backyard. Wherever

your gardening practice may be, begin by turning the soil and planting seeds. Check with a local nursery to find out what would work well in your climate.

Begin by planting the seeds, following package instructions. Keep a small gardening journal that allows you to note how many seeds you plant, how long it takes for them to sprout, and how the sprouts fare once the plants begin to mature. As you check the plants, water, and thin the seedlings, pay attention to what you learn as you go along.

2. The gift of humility allows us to recognize that we are part of a vast and diverse creation, and that in our neighbors we are gifted with Christ's presence in a variety of disguises. One way to enlarge your awareness of being connected to this larger whole, this macrocosm, is to volunteer at a local hunger ministry. If you have not had this opportunity, search out a place where you have the chance to prepare and/or serve food to those in need and to come to know some of the people present. As you engage with those receiving the food, offer this prayer silently: "The Christ in me bless the Christ in you."

Over the course of several weeks, as you continue to offer time in this hunger ministry, note in your journal what you become aware of through this prayer. Be attentive to the tensions, questions, and feelings that the experience brings.

You may want to spend some time with a trusted friend talking about your experience.

3. The practice of humility brings us to an awareness of our own sharp tendencies to judge others. Roberta Bondi has observed, "No one is in a position to look down on another from a superior height because of her or his hard work or piety or mental superiority. We are all vulnerable, all limited, and we each have a different struggle only God is in a position to judge."[33]

Reflect on the last twenty-four hours. As you remember your thoughts and actions, where do you notice that you were judging another? Is there a person that you consistently judge? What do criticize about that person? Is there any similarity in your own personality? Can you imagine a different way to engage that person? If you feel really stuck, ask for help: "Gracious God, I want to stop judging this person."

In the days ahead, attempt to notice the moments when you judge another. Try to catch yourself, and ask for God's guidance in seeing that person with eyes of mercy.

Closing Prayer

O God, in Christ you emptied yourself to become our friend; may I grow in your own humility, befriending all you have made. Amen.

CHAPTER 8

Showing Up Daily, or Becoming an Ascetic

"Those who are great athletes must contend against strong enemies."

–Amma Syncletica[34]

At the period in history in which the desert became filled with men and women seeking God, the church had incorporated the ideal of *ascesis* from Greek life and culture, a term that referred to the physical preparation of athletes. As these Christians understood it, an ascetical life was one in which disciplined training and preparation were also necessary to "run the race" of faith. We know this imagery from Saint Paul, who writes, "Athletes exercise self-control in all things; they do it to receive a perishable wreath, but we an imperishable one" (1 Corinthians 9:25). At the same time, a good athlete knows the wisdom of balance and moderation, of not doing things to excess. An athlete who loves her practice will come to it daily and allow it to inform the rest of her daily life. Lessons learned while warming up, while seeking to train her body, while supporting her body for the sport or game, translate to other dimensions of her life.

Embodying Love

"Asceticism" is a word that works well with a faith in an Incarnate Lord, a Lord who lived a human life, a Lord who came to us in a human body. In Jesus, God experiences human life from the inside out—breathing, digesting, getting tired, needing sleep, having a headache. God's incarnation in Jesus calls us to take our own physical, embodied life as a gift. That incarnation hallows human flesh in all of its physicality. As a friend of mine used to say, "God loves human bodies so much that he just had to have one."

At its best, the Christian way from the very beginning understood the body as God's own handiwork. The desert ammas' teachings in this regard understand that the spiritual life is *always* a physical, embodied life. Their intent was to be mindful of our physical needs in such a way that those needs served the love of God and love of neighbor. Some of their sayings may sound dualistic to us (teachings that view the body and matter as evil, and only the soul as good). On the contrary, the ammas were combating precisely that kind of dualistic thinking in their own context. Their sayings would have been a challenge to the Manicheans, the followers of a dualistic tradition in their day. The ammas invite us to understand the body both as a gift from God and as the vehicle through which we live out the Great Commandment. Thus, how much I eat and how much I sleep may reveal my inability to love either myself or others. How I fast may reveal my lack of trust in God as I indulge in heroics. The good news is that the body is inescapably the locus of God's transforming grace—not in the sense that our bodies become worthy of a fashion cover shoot, but in the sense that all acts of love are *acts*—they require incarnation in the world.

Ascetical theology focuses on the body not because the body is evil or corrupt (a frequent misunderstanding) but because it must be honed and prepared for the task at hand—for the running of the race of faith. For the athlete, training is a way to achieve running the best race he or she can. For the desert mothers and fathers, ascetical training was a tool. For us, Christian ascetical training can be a means of deepening fidelity and practice with the hope of becoming united with Christ, that he might dwell in us and we in him.

Discipline and Love

The desert ammas had regular discipline that was oriented toward the goal of learning to love. When you combine the terms "discipline" and "love," you are no longer talking about romantic love or love for a particular place or custom. Those who went to the desert entered a kind of school, a school in which the practice of loving as God loves was the primary and foundational lesson.[35] Ascetical training was, to use a current term, "lifetime learning." This is training from which you never graduate. You keep showing up, practicing, integrating, and growing. The commitment to the practice of this kind of love is not lived out with grim and self-focused determination, but with a gracious joy. Roberta Bondi points out, "One sixth-century writer who took the suffering of Jesus on the cross very seriously spoke of him being 'crucified in the divine cheerfulness.'"[36] This wedding of love and discipline allows us to begin to delight in God's desire to make us real, to bring us to the fullness of our humanity, to encourage us to grow continually in God's love and service. And to do that, we need the principles learned from athletes of all kinds—the willingness to be in training, to tend to the needs of our bodies, to learn and to practice, to be ever grateful for "teammates" and companions on the way.

A young friend of mine, Terry, is a runner. She has run out of sheer enjoyment since she was in middle school. For Terry, the practice of running has become a way of offering worship. Like the runner training for the Olympics in the movie *Chariots of Fire*, when Terry runs, she recognizes that she was created to run and she feels God's pleasure in her running.

I, on the other hand, am not a runner. I never have been and never will be. For me, the gift of the language of the ascetical life is that it offers wisdom with regard to simply showing up for life and for prayer. It offers insight about moderation and balance and about the ways in which regular practice forms us in the walk of faith. Just as an athlete needs to learn the importance of regular rhythms of practice, of repetition of basic drills, and of prioritizing in order to have the time to work out, we "desert athletes" also need those basic disciplines.

Showing Up for Practice

As is the case with athletic training, yoga or tennis or tai chi, regular practice is essential. It is important to show up for practice. So it is with the ascetical life. Those of us who think we can fix things overnight, lose thirty pounds in thirty days, or learn to speak French fluently in six weeks, have very little notion of the depth of transformation that may be achieved by regular training in the Christian life. We tend to approach the life of faith as if it were another fad rather than a way of becoming new. An athlete will tell you that training requires enough regularity to create muscle memory, so that our muscles "remember" what is expected of them—in yoga, they remember the stretch; in soccer, they remember the running, dodging, and kicking. This muscle memory is particular to the athlete and the training regimen, just as spiritual practice will have its particular expressions in the life of both the person and the community.

Since human beings are easily bored, we tend to think something is wrong with what we are doing if we get bored. On the contrary, our incessant hunger for overstimulation and overwork keep us from deepening practice—whether that practice is tai chi, walking, or silent prayer. Our culture, dominated as it is by advertising, encourages us to drop any practice as soon as another comes along that is more interesting. We seem to have made the assumption that the spiritual life (always embodied) has to be marked by being "interesting." I have asked myself what we mean by that, and often we mean that it needs to be "stimulating." We create inhumane rhythms and expectations by trying to do everything quickly instead of choosing one or two things to do well. With their awareness of this particular spiritual pitfall, the ammas would be confounded by our rushing from one activity to another. They would ask us what is underneath the hurry and our perpetual quest for more stimulation, more experience. The teachings from the desert tell us that this kind of restless boredom is often caused by physical and spiritual exhaustion. The ammas' counsel to us would be to rest, to be still, to allow ourselves time to stop. Imagine that, a Christian spiritual way that counsels rest when we are exhausted, and even considers exhaustion to be a dangerous spiritual condition. The

It is often the case that when we persevere through episodes of boredom, we will break through to a deeper level of discernment and openness. And, more to the point, it is often when we feel that dispirited restlessness that we most *need* to rest, to cease from doing, simply to be quiet and breathe.

Julianne had been praying at lunch during her work day for several years. Then, for no apparent reason, her prayer began to dry up. The habit that had initially brought her joy and peace began to feel irritating and dull. The sameness of the daily experience of prayer was not what she had hoped for, and she longed for that first delight in being in prayer and sensing God's presence.

Julianne found herself creating reasons not to pray. She was too uneasy with the boredom. It was easier to do something else than sit still and listen. Her spiritual director, after listening and helping Julianne discern some of what was happening within her spirit, suggested that Julianne not give up her noonday prayer time. Rather, keeping the same time and space, she began to put aside the oral prayers she had been accustomed to using, the prayers that had become like stale toast. Julianne simply began to sit and listen. For ten minutes at first, then fifteen, then twenty, Julianne sat in the presence of God. Her director encouraged her to rest in God's presence. "To rest?" Julianne asked. "Is that okay?" She began to uncover her own anxiety about performing for God (and herself) in prayer. She began to let herself be still, to trust God enough to not *do* anything. Her restlessness gave way to rest; her practice deepened because she kept showing up. Like a good athlete, she noticed when she was "off her game" and sought the advice of her "coach"—in this case, her spiritual director. By staying in her cell, seeking a "word" from her director, and staying with the boredom, Julianne entered a new phase in her prayer without being seduced by something more interesting.

Suggestions for Reflection and Prayer

1. Many of us need a gentle, physical practice that allows us to honor our bodies. If you are not accustomed to this, you may want to experiment with walking or simple stretching. In the last year, I have begun to practice chi gung (or qigong), a form of movement used throughout China for healing and wellness. Yoga has also been very beneficial in my own experience. This discipline for the body is not intended to "whip it into shape," but to honor our physical existence as a God-given gift. For the time of the walking or stretching, our attention is more on our breath and our muscles than on our work or phone calls. I know several women who have discovered that their regular time for

swimming or yoga or running is more and more a time of being aware of God's presence in the working of their bodies—in the very fact of being able to breathe, to digest, to move, to think.

If you are just getting started, try to avoid heroics. Begin with small increments of time, in regular rhythm, and build slowly. As you show up for this practice, begin to notice the various processes that you take for granted: lungs that exchange carbon dioxide for oxygen, a heart that beats regularly, a stomach that transforms food into energy. Even if you are living with an illness of some kind, give thanks for what is working!

2. John Chryssavgis observes, "There are times, Syncletica would feel, when the problems in our life are of themselves sufficient ascetic struggle, if endured thankfully. There is no need to overburden the body with further labors of fasting."[37] If you are in a time in your life in which you are beset by difficulties, you may not need to impose any further discipline. Your life as it is presently unfolding may provide more than enough discipline. If, for example, you have a family member who is gravely ill, or you have recently been through a rough move from one city to another, each day will provide its own ascetical practice. Beware of adding undue pressure to an already stressful context. If you find yourself in this kind of circumstance, your primary practice may be to discover ways to rest, to play, and to enjoy what you can daily.

3. Athletes know that you cannot run a mile without gradually having practiced to run that distance. The desert mothers were aware that the life of ascetical practice had to be crafted patiently, with steady and persevering attention. In their lives, a fairly simple structure was possible. There were no children or lovers in the desert, because everyone was living a monastic life. They did not have the added complications of family, although they were committed to being part of a community and to hospitality.

Ask yourself if you generally feel tired and stressed. If that is the case, begin to build in periods of rest. This could be taking ten minutes at the office to turn off the computer and not answer the phone, and then to sit still, breathing with kind attention to your body. It could be sitting in the dark in your home, doing nothing more than breathing and being still for fifteen minutes. If your fatigue is the primary characteristic of your life, you may also need to see a physician for a check-up to make sure that there is not an organic cause.

While sitting in silence, you do not need to pray verbally. If you feel the need to pray in words, in addition to praying by being still and listening, pick a simple phrase such as "Breathe in me, breath of God," and repeat it softly as you sit.

Closing Prayer

Merciful and ever-living God, for you alone my soul in silence waits. In you I find my rest, and my body shall rest in hope. Amen.

CHAPTER 9

Living a Dedicated Life

The Ongoing Practice of Listening and Choosing

"In truth, lack of proportion always corrupts."

–Amma Syncletica[38]

The desert mothers offer us one example of what a dedicated life looks like. Their daily regimen included early morning prayer, silence, praying the psalms, manual labor, and simple eating. They sought to live in a way that was simple enough that they would not confuse the trappings of their lives for life itself.

As we begin to learn more about their way of living out their faith, we need to notice something of primary significance: these women lived their lives creatively. Practicing discernment, seeking guidance from spiritual companions, listening to their lives, these ammas followed discipline in order to love well and creatively. They dedicated their lives to living out the Great Commandment. In the face of all sorts of cultural assumptions that women were creatures whose wills were corrupt or fallible, the desert mothers made choices that they prayed about and acted upon. "Big deal," you may be thinking. "What difference does that make?" In every age, in every society, some choices are encouraged and expected. I am of an age and social location that when I was finishing studies at the University of Texas at Austin, I realized that I should get married pretty quickly after I finished my degree. At the time, in Texas, it was normative and expected that a woman in her early twenties would get married, have children, and be a good spouse. Doing anything differently was hard work. In my case, the cultural script included the blessing of a long marriage with two sons, but for other women of my age, these familial and social expectations to marry right out of college resulted in marriages that were wrong for both parties. Other women in their mid-fifties like me may have made career choices that also fit in with social expectations, but later they permitted themselves to change course and train for a vocation more in line with their innate gifts and abilities. My point is that all of us have to come to terms with social and cultural norms and expectations. If we make choices that are reflected upon and undertaken with care and guidance, we can continue to live with discernment.

You may have made some choices along the way that were accepted and blessed by your family, your culture, and your religious tradition. Or you may have taken an alternative route and intentionally gone against the social grain in your own choosing. Or your own circumstances may have put you at variance with what was expected, and you are well aware of the discomfort that can cause.

In the case of the desert mothers, we observe that they opted out of the usual ways of living as a woman and a wife. Historian and scholar Peter Brown has observed that in the second century, the average life expectancy of a citizen of the Roman Empire was twenty-five years. Very few women lived beyond the age of fifty. There was tremendous social and political expectation that young women (young teenagers) would marry and produce citizens for the empire. Brown remarks, "The pressure on the young women was inexorable."[39]

We notice that these ammas found in the gospel the freedom to answer the call of God to be different and to be authentic. They left behind what they were socialized to be and believe and went toward a new life. As they departed for the desert, they were entering a great unknown, both in terms of landscape and in terms of their own souls. They dedicated their lives to embodying the Great Commandment. In choosing to be trained in the way of the Great Commandment, the desert ammas sought a freedom from social and cultural assumptions. They gave themselves to the love of God and love of neighbor, a truly countercultural way of being and living. How might we, who live so many centuries later, follow this desert way as the ammas did, seeking the inner freedom that allows us to walk in loving service?

Find the Middle Way

While the sayings and stories from some desert elders include examples that would lead us to question their view of the human body, such as extremes of fasting or other forms of self-mortification, Amma Syncletica counseled moderation and balance. Her sayings call us to live in a way that avoids extremes—extremes of fasting or eating, of being alone, or being in community. The undergirding wisdom from Amma Syncletica calls us to notice where our lives are out of kilter, where we see frenetic or anxious energy and behavior in our lives. She invites us to notice where we are sacrificing ourselves to the insatiable gods of work, competition, control, ambition, or social pressure.

One mistake we can make is to understand the way of Christian faith to be narrow and perfectionist. In the Gospel of Matthew, in the verse that is often translated "Be perfect, therefore, as your heavenly Father is perfect" (5:48), we find Jesus calling his followers to a life of faith that is full and complete. The Greek word translated as "perfect" implies that we were created by God and for God, and that when we live from that faith, our intentions change. Perfection in this sense has to do with our orienting our lives toward the God from whom we come and to whom we will return. Perfection has to do with knowing that our deepest desires are not satisfied by ambition, or material success, or even a fine family. While we may have those goals, for the Christian, they are always secondary to the goal of the Great Commandment.

Following the Great Commandment, learning to love anew, requires daily practice. Small movements of kindness, generosity, compassion, self-control, gentleness, patience, and joy, carried out mindfully in the course of daily living, shape us in the shape of Christ. We become, over time, more open to the possibilities of making choices that honor our lives as women created in the image and likeness of God. We become less susceptible to the messages of media and culture that imply that we all must be well-dressed, thin as a rail, and perfect mothers and spouses and executives. Instead, we begin to discover the real and lively diversity of women seeking to discover and to encourage the God-given fruitfulness of our lives.

This kind of ascesis may entail some kinds of letting go and giving up. We may discover that for our own health, sanity, and growth in love, we need to be mindful about how we internalize images of women taken from advertising. We may discover that we need to spend less time at the computer and more time volunteering. Or we may find that we are volunteering so much that we have no idea who we are any more. Desert spirituality offers us a way to honor the singularity of each life, while also recognizing that those lives are inextricably bound together by divine love. In practicing the moderation and balance counseled by Amma Syncletica, we are invited to pay gentle attention to our own lives, to our own communities and families, and to find rhythms that embody active loving. This is a process that unfolds under a gently attentive gaze as we look at the patterns of our lives—daily, monthly, yearly.

The desert mothers invite us to enter into training, a kind of schooling of body, mind, and spirit. This training and practice is regular, and it is lived in small moments. Ascetical practice, ascetical training, is always lived out in the daily sphere. If it becomes heroic and ego centered, it is no longer about living a dedicated, balanced life. Years ago, a woman I knew complained to me that she was not being faithful to her fast for Lent. When I began to ask about her chosen discipline for that season before Holy Week and Easter, I discovered that she had set up terribly rigorous expectations for herself in regard to fasting. The focus of the fast was no longer God, but herself. She was taking a kind of secret pride in just how much she could prove to God by giving up so much. Her fast was not offered in love, but out of a kind of desperation to prove herself. This is not what Amma Syncletica would bless as a practice of moderation. The walk of faith is not a competition; it is a company, walking together, encouraging one another, tending each other gently.

Live Your Life as Ascetical Practice

Another mistake that we can make in the spiritual life is assuming that what is "spiritual" is somehow separate from what we do in the course of a normal day. In this view, care of family, daily work, and the round of errands and carpools are all outside the realm of spiritual practice and care. The ammas would disagree strongly with this. It is not the case that there is a "spiritual life" that is somehow distinct from the daily routine. Nor is there a "spiritual life" that in and of itself is somehow more worthy than life in its minutiae and dailiness.

All of life is an ascetical practice. What do I mean by that? Very simply, I mean that the entire fabric of our lives is woven together with God's life. There is no moment, no hour, no day when God is not with us. The ascetical practice for those of us who are not monastics, while of the same Spirit, is different in expression. We are called upon to practice love in the lives we already live. We are invited to be alert for the opportunities to notice the Presence that is with us every moment, in every place. We are invited to bring a different intention to our relationships, to our work, to our leisure.

Our intention has to do with being "perfect" in the sense of seeking fulfillment in God. If my intent during the course of a day is to be awake and mindful of God's presence and direction in the course of a day, that intention will change the way in which I encounter others. It will alter the way in which I encounter the events of the day as they unfold. Life becomes less something to be endured or to be grabbed. Daily life becomes the very habitat of God, where God chooses to live and move. Each day may have its own moments of theophany—its own moments when God's mysterious interaction with all that is breaks through and shakes us out of our complacency and fear.

For Mattie, this kind of transformation took place within the context of raising small children. Mattie had been an accountant. She was good at her profession, but she also wanted to stay home with her children. For her, finding a way to stay home and work part time became a kind of ascesis, a discipline. Did she miss her professional life? Yes. Was she glad that she was spending time with her young children? Yes. Part of her practice, her ascetical training, has been to learn to live with that tension. Mattie has come to understand that this contradiction of wanting both to be with her children and to have her professional life will require regular discernment and prayer. For the moment, she is noticing her desire to return to work while also recognizing the increased strain on her household budget. She is looking at the details with care, attention, and prayer, and listening for guidance in her life, from her family, and from her spiritual director.

Suggestions for Practicing Moderation and Balance

1. Often we are unaware of how we spend our time each day. We come to the end of a day and wonder why nothing that we started out to do has gotten accomplished. The desert tradition would tell us to be a bit wary of so little attention given to what we do.

Start keeping a record of how you spend your time. Write down the "givens"—what has to be done within your particular context. Be mindful of the "givens" that you might overlook—things like grocery shopping, carpool duty, and laundry. Notice, over time, how your time, daily and weekly, is spent.

As you keep this record, you may find that you are surprised by what actually occurs in the course of a day. Notice the interruptions. Notice how your life unfolds each day.

Once you have this record, (and you will need to wait a couple of weeks before you can proceed with this part of the reflection), ask yourself:

Is this too much?
What parts are "givens" and will not change soon?
Where are the tensions?
What is missing?
How, when, where did I experience God's presence in the midst of these activities?
If I could change one detail, what would it be? (We often make the mistake of trying to change everything at once, which is a set-up for disappointment. Pick something that could realistically be changed, perhaps by simply no longer doing it.)

2. Using the insights from the previous exercise, go back to the tensions. Notice the places in your life in which you may have two good desires pulling in different directions, as

Mattie did with regard to her children and her professional life. Without seeking an immediate solution (because this isn't necessarily a problem—these areas of tension often call for prayer and reflection, not quick resolution), try to discover the nuance of the tension. On the surface, in Mattie's case, there was the obvious tension between young children and her professional life. On a deeper level, Mattie continues to discover a variety of insights—how she perceives herself if she is not earning a salary and whether that perception is accurate, what her life with the small children is teaching her, how her life has shifted since she began working in her mid-twenties.

As you notice the underlying nuances and issues, be patient if you do not have ready answers. This process is not so much about finding answers as it is about patiently uncovering the God-given rhythm and balance for your life within its particular necessities and requirements.

3. One of the strongest scriptural metaphors for returning to moderation is that of pruning. Jesus says in John 15:2, "Every branch that bears fruit he prunes to make it bear more fruit." As a gardener, I know that this kind of pruning is necessary for the health of the plant. From time to time, I have to prune my own life. I have to carefully cut back what has bloomed and gone to seed, and I have to cut off the "dead branches." Last summer, as my family sought to find a rhythm and balance in living with my older son's illness, one important pruning took place with regard to e-mail. I carefully unsubscribed from a variety of e-mail newsletters from charitable organizations. Those newsletters, in and of themselves, are good things. However, in my particular circumstances, I needed clear space in order to tend to the details of my son's treatments. I was overloaded with medical details and had no room for more information.

"Unsubscribing" became a metaphor for pruning away activities that, while good in and of themselves, were simply too much within the context of living with my son's illness.

Again returning to the insights gained from the first exercise, ask yourself if there are things from which you could "unsubscribe." Are there activities that have become burdens or are simply one thing too many? Allow yourself to imagine what might happen if you unsubscribe.

If you are ready, begin by letting go of at least one activity that seems either superfluous or unnecessary.

4. Possibly, as you looked over the pattern of your days, you felt that something was missing. Perhaps you discovered that you desire more time for being with friends. Or perhaps you find that you are so active that you are missing time to simply sit and reflect. If you felt that some essential aspect of your life is being crowded or untended, ask yourself what might be dropped so that you could tend that part of your life. By simply noticing that something is missing, you will begin to honor that "branch" of your life that God has created to bear fruit. Over time, ask in prayer for guidance about nurturing this branch, and offering the fruit for the larger community.

Closing Prayer

O gracious Christ, you are the vine and we are the branches. Grant me the wisdom and the care to tend the fruit of my life, to live with dedication and devotion that the desires you have placed within me may be fulfilled. Amen.

CHAPTER 10

Becoming Fully Human

"It is good to give alms for people's sake. Even if it is done only to please others, through it one can begin to seek to please God."

–*Amma Sarah*[40]

In the fourth century, the desert of Egypt became like a city. The desert was full of men and women seeking to live out the Great Commandment. There were also pilgrims and seekers going to the ammas and abbas to seek counsel, to ask, "Give me a word." In addition, there were tourists and curiosity seekers who came to gawk and to sightsee, desirous of claiming that they had witnessed the holy desert elders for themselves. When I look at the pictures of the sparse and lunar terrain in which this activity was occurring, I can understand the context out of which Amma Sarah is speaking. On the one hand, she is reiterating a truth that is deep within Judeo-Christian roots—a sense that we are all in this life together, and that we are called to care for one another, especially for those who are hungry, thirsty, lonely, naked, sick, imprisoned (Matthew 25:35–46). The desert elders needed to care for each other, but they also needed to care for the many who came to doors of their cells and their communities, in some cases seeking healing and hospitality.

Amma Sarah's saying is mindful of the variety of intentions underlying the giving of alms in whatever form. We may give in order to feel better about ourselves or to create a reputation for generosity. We may give out of guilt or we may give out of abundance. Whatever the intention, the fact remains that the act of giving is a way to begin to please God.

Notice that Sarah assumes that we would desire to please God. In this day and age, that assumption might be questionable, but the same would have been true during Sarah's time. She is aware of interplay between faith and action. Faith forms and informs action. The reverse is also true. In the parlance of Twelve Step recovery, sometimes we walk the talk and sometimes we talk the walk. Both need to happen for us to grow in awareness that our place in the world is one of many places, that each of those places has its own value, and that all the places are interconnected. Each of those places is linked through God in Christ and is part of a living, interdependent whole. When you give alms, on the one hand, you act to meet the need of your brother or sister, your neighbor in Christ. On the other hand, you are implicitly opening your awareness to those who have no direct claim on you. Each act of giving offers you the grace to be moved off center, to allow God to be at the center of all that you are and all that you have. When this begins to happen, you become more fully human. You grow in the image and likeness of God. You practice having eyes to see and ears to hear, and then you act on what you perceive in love. You begin to allow the living Christ to shape your life so that it resembles his.

The desert ammas were subversives. They were subversives as the gospel is subversive, as Jesus reminds us that we are not fully human unless we keep an awareness of those who are hungry, thirsty, lonely, sick, naked, imprisoned. Not only are we called to awareness, we are also called to allow the living God to work in and through us in love, so that the awareness may be translated into compassionate action. John Chryssavgis writes, "The desert is a place of spiritual revolution, not of personal retreat. It is a place of inner protest, not outward peace. It is a place of deep encounter, not of superficial escape. It is a place of repentance, not recuperation."[41]

Those women who went to the desert chose to take radical steps. As they decided to live in a landscape where reputation and success and even holiness did not matter, they began to be delivered from the distress of putting themselves before God and neighbor. In the steady reconfiguration of priorities offered by that landscape and by that tradition, the ammas and the abbas began to see themselves as part of the *kosmos*, as participants in a vast and beautiful universe created, sustained, and redeemed by the ever-living God. As the desert allowed them to recognize their own littleness and the shortness of human life, the ammas were able to allow the love of God to "heal the dullness of [their] blinded sight."[42] The world became a manger full of holy children whose lives were threatened, and the universe became a burning bush, holy ground through which the living God speaks to those who will listen.

The desert allowed these holy women to rediscover a deep truth: we are less than human without each other. We are less than human without recognition of the gift of the world. We are less than human when we take for granted full bellies and healthy bodies. Ultimately, because the ammas were schooled in the love of God and love of neighbor, they urge us to look beyond ourselves, to practice an embodied spirituality that always questions whether my well-being comes at the cost of another's scarcity.[43]

Thus, when we fast (whether that be from food or noise or busyness or buying too much), our fast is not only for our own health and deepening love; it is offered for the life of the world. When we fast from mean-spirited conversation and from the need to always be in control and think ourselves to be right, we are allowing open space in which God's healing silence can bring forth something new, if we give it time and care. When we fast from hurry and frenetic, nonstop rushing, we not only allow the distended stress of our bodies and souls to heal. We also practice one of the most subversive acts in this society: rest in God, trusting that God's own re-creating and restoring grace will be sufficient for the tasks at hand. We put aside the addictive behavior of working as if everything depended upon our efforts, and allow real questions to surface. What is enough? What does this family really need? Why am I never feeling caught up? What happened to "free time"?

The ammas will not answer those questions for you. They will tell you that the questions are an essential part of discovering who you are and who you are called to be. They will tell you that when you stop, when you notice your own hungers and thirsts, your own loneliness and sadness, your own life, you will begin to move toward the truth in love. You will begin the struggle to birth your own life, the life shaped by the love of God, the life that is singularly marked by your creative choosing in love.

Suggestions for Prayer and Practice

1. Reflect on what need in the world seems to invite your care and attention. This could be hunger, the environment, AIDS—there are any number of possibilities. Once you have decided on one need, connect with an organization that addresses it. For example, if you feel called to address world hunger, you might begin by connecting with Oxfam, an organization that seeks to bring governmental policy in line with the needs of the hungry.

Choose to give regularly to the organization, thereby becoming a part of a larger group. Pray for the organization and for the people it serves.

If there is a local branch of the organization, and you feel called to do so, begin attending local gatherings focused on the needs in your community.

2. In your own community, perhaps through your faith community, begin to notice the hungry, thirsty, unclothed, lonely, and imprisoned people. Seek to discover if you are being invited to directly address any of those needs—whether through monetary donation, regular participation, or in offering your gifts to the ministries that help meet those needs. Perhaps, for example, you sense a desire to be mindful of the victims of family violence in your community. In addition to supporting centers that help those who have suffered from domestic violence, you could help with fundraising, work as a volunteer, or find ways to give the victims needed visibility so that the larger community knows of their presence and is moved to act. As you participate in this connection and giving of the "alms of your life," remember to pray the prayer you learned in an earlier chapter, "May the Christ in me bless the Christ in you."

3. Sometimes, it is easy to forget that we are guests traveling in a vast universe not of our own making. On a cloudless night, go outside and spend time gazing at the stars; if you live in a city, practice this on retreat. As you gaze at the stars and the moon,

breathe gently and repeat, "The one who made the Pleiades and Orion" (Amos 5:8).

Closing Prayer

Living God, in you I live and move and have my being; may I never forget that all that is created is in you, and grant me the grace to live from that truth. Amen.

CHAPTER 11

The Desert Is for All of Us

When I was in high school, during the summer of 1966, my family took the long trip west to go to California as tourists. We were living in San Antonio, Texas, a city marked by hills and oak trees, rivers and creeks. I'd lived there all my life. So of course, the prospect of heading toward the Pacific was exciting, even if it did mean squeezing all six of us in the car.

As we headed west on Interstate 10, leaving the Texas hill country behind, a vast open space began to open up. The farther west we went, the emptier the landscape became. For the first time in my seventeen years, I was getting a taste of the desert. Our car began to feel even smaller than it was—as if it were a tiny beetle in the midst of all that land, all that sky. As we entered New Mexico, though the appearance of the land changed dramatically, it was still dry, arid beyond anything I had known or imagined. We went to White Sands National Monument and played in the dunes. We watched the colors shift and ripple as sunset approached, like purple *rebozos* settling on the mesas.

New Mexico, Arizona, Nevada, Southern California. Desert everywhere we looked.

We spent one night in Las Vegas. My favorite memory is the swimming pool. It was as if my whole being was screaming for water, for some reassurance that there was water even in the midst of all that dry land. I remember swimming the length of the pool underwater (it was a small motel pool, so this was not a big feat). Something in me wanted to be completely submerged, to be like an otter at home in the water. From my early years, I was drawn to water. I was not drawn to the desert.

I had a copy of Mary Stewart's *The Moonspinners* with me, and I read it twice. So many boring hours spent in the car—the desert did not offer any diversions for the eye or for the spirit. We drove and drove without seeing trees or lakes or people. My teenage self had the sense to know that this was not an environment that would be easy to live in. Even then, I realized it was hard to hide from myself in the desert. I remember the palpable relief when we began to make our way past Needles, California, now just hours from Los Angeles and Disneyland. We savored California and all the delights of driving north on Highway 1 with the Pacific on our left. We marveled at a shoreline that was completely rocky (the Texas beaches are all sand), and shivered with astonishment when our feet were splashed by the cold Pacific. We watched the fog come in while staying in San Francisco, and made the acquaintance of the seals on Fisherman's Wharf.

And then we started home.

Through the desert.

One more time.

It was as unnerving for me as it had been heading west. I worried that we would have a flat tire in the middle of nowhere, or that the car would overheat. I wished we could roll the windows down instead of using the air conditioner. But most of all, I just wanted to be in a landscape that offered a friendly, familiar environment. The desert disconcerted me. It took a long time before the stark contrasts of cold and hot, dark and light became attractive, before I could perceive the beauty of the stillness, the lack of diversion, the vast empty space.

So I am surprised at midlife to discover in myself an affinity for the Christian writings from the deserts of Egypt from the early days of the faith. It's more than affinity, actually. These writings have become a tonic. Sayings and stories, this tradition was initially oral, handed down from one person to another. It bears some similarity to the proverbs that surface in every folk culture around the world. One seeker asks for guidance and direction. Another offers a bit of wisdom—sometimes like a proverb, sometimes in a little story. In that sense, the wisdom from this desert tradition is gleaned from observation and from experience. The words have the flavor of comfort food without the fat. By that I mean that the tradition comforts as the Holy Spirit comforts, by strengthening the inner person to know the height and the breadth, the depth and the width of the love of Christ (Ephesians 3:18). In scriptural terms, the word in Hebrew that is translated as "comfort" could also mean "strengthen." The comfort offered by the living God is not the comfort of a greeting card; it is the comfort of truth spoken to a particular person in a particular context.

This desert tradition grew out of a landscape that is lunar in appearance and forbidding in its rocky spareness. The men and women who went to the desert in those early times to dedicate their lives to Christ seem strange and remote to us. It is hardly possible for us to imagine our way into their culture and society. At the same time, their awareness of the central and basic practices necessary for embodying the life in Christ come to us as good teaching and faithful living. We are given compassionate glimpses into the struggle within the human heart—the struggle to live genuinely, to wake up to the reality of our creaturely nature, to be less selfish, to know that we will die. The desert mothers and fathers help us remember the basics of how to become a real human being: practice respect, learn to seek guidance, do not judge your neighbor, remember that others are involved when you make choices, take yourself as lightly as possible. Daily practice, focused on what matters in the long run, shapes each of us into true human beings, marked by the glory of God, created in the divine image and likeness. An attentiveness that stays alert for the living Word speaking in and through the most ordinary of moments undergirds the practice—an attentiveness that is cultivated in the garden of silence, solitude, and stillness.

The desert tradition is not for cowards or spiritual gadabouts. It is a tradition that cuts to the chase. It is a tradition that does not tend to fluff or appearances. It may be that it is a tradition peculiarly suited for the dilemmas of midlife, as we begin to confront our numbered days and to recognize that we will not be alive forever. These ammas have offered us the most basic of spiritual lessons. There is a simplicity and lucidity in this tradition that calls us away from focusing on prayer technique or doctrine or ideology. The desert doesn't really care about our opinions. The desert will call us to be real, to ditch all pretenses, and to be mindful of loving God, neighbor, and self. The desert will teach us in its own way if we have the sense to go there and listen.

Throughout our Judeo-Christian history, the desert has been a place of encounter, a place in which the unfathomable mystery of God meets our creaturely selves. From the Israelite sojourn of forty years to Jesus' temptation in the wilderness, scripture gives us the precedent of desert revelation. Moses looks at the bush, and it burns without being consumed. The angels minister to Jesus amid the rocky wilds. The stories tell us this: in a sparse landscape, it is hard to fool ourselves. In an empty natural setting, we come face to face with our own limitations and mortality and with the fact of our creaturely dependence. The desert spaces help us strip away illusions and lies. In that empty space, the voice of God that thunders over the waters may thunder inside the human soul. The voice of God that comes in the still small voice to Elijah may whisper so softly that the footfalls of the lizard obscure the sound.

The fourth-century Christians who wished to dedicate themselves fully to Christ went to the desert. In doing so, they were following the pattern established by their ancestors in the faith. The scriptures themselves point to the barren places as places of grace and mercy. As the psalmist writes, "God turns a desert into pools of water, a parched land into springs of water" (Psalm 107:35). The desert is a place of transformation, transformation often occurring when we least expect it and coming to us in forms that we would never have chosen.

The tradition that was formed in the desert landscape speaks profoundly to those times in our lives that feel like a desolate valley, like a place with scant sources of water, like a harsh environment in which daily survival requires every ounce of our energy. We all go through life passages in which these images of desert, dryness, stony paths, desolate space, speak profoundly to our own circumstance. In my own life, cancer, other illness, deaths of loved ones, tectonic shifts in professional identity, economic change, have all been moments when desert spirituality spoke to the immediate situation of my life. When I felt panic rise up, the desert tradition counseled me to breathe. When I was choked by anxiety, the desert tradition coaxed me to open up, to seek a friend, to say what was in my heart. When I felt trapped or cornered, the desert elders helped me name what needed to be named. And when

I thought I was going to die, they reminded me that each tomb is eventually emptied.

May these ammas travel with you in your own deserts, offering their guidance, love, and companionship.

Suggestions for Further Reading

Desert Spirituality

Bondi, Roberta C. *To Love as God Loves.* Philadelphia: Fortress, 1987.

Chryssavgis, John. *In the Heart of the Desert: The Spirituality of the Desert Fathers and Mothers.* Bloomington, IN: World Wisdom, 2003.

Forman, Mary, O.S.B. *Praying with the Desert Mothers.* Collegeville, MN: Liturgical Press, 2005.

Keller, David G. R. *Oasis of Wisdom: The Worlds of the Desert Fathers and Mothers.* Collegeville, MN: Liturgical Press, 2005.

Nouwen, Henri J. M. *The Way of the Heart.* New York: Ballantine, 1981.

Swan, Laura. *The Forgotten Desert Mothers: Sayings, Lives, and Stories of Early Christian Women.* New York: Paulist Press, 2001.

Ward, Benedicta, S.L.G., trans., *The Sayings of the Desert Fathers: The Alphabetical Collection.* Kalamazoo, MI: Cistercian Publications, 1975.

Discernment

Farrington, Debra. *Hearing with the Heart: A Gentle Guide to Discerning God's Will for Your Life.* San Francisco: Jossey-Bass, 2003.

Palmer, Parker. *Let Your Life Speak: Listening for the Voice of Vocation.* San Francisco: Jossey-Bass, 2000.

Silence and Prayer

McPherson, C. W. *Keeping Silence: Christian Practices for Entering Stillness.* Harrisburg, PA: Morehouse, 2002.

Vest, Norvene. *No Moment Too Small: Rhythms of Silence, Prayer, and Holy Reading.* Cambridge, MA: Cowley, 1994.

Notes

Chaper 1: Introduction: Where Are the Mothers?

1. Roberta Bondi, *To Love as God Loves* (Philadelphia: Fortress, 1987), 7.

2. See, for example, Susanna Elm, *Virgins of God: The Making of Asceticism in Late Antiquity* (Oxford: Clarendon, 1994); Anne Jensen, *God's Self-Confident Daughters: Early Christianity and the Liberation of Women* (Louisville, KY: Westminster John Knox, 1996); Susanne Heine, *Women and Early Christianity: A Reappraisal*, trans. John Bowden (Minneapolis: Augsburg, 1988).

3. Laura Swan, *The Forgotten Desert Mothers* (New York: Paulist Press, 2001), 3.

4. Roberta Bondi, *To Love as God Loves* and *To Pray and To Love* (Minneapolis: Augsburg Fortress, 1991).

5. Mary Forman, O.S.B., *Praying with the Desert Mothers* (Collegeville, MN: Liturgical Press, 2005).

Chapter 2: Desert Spirituality

6. Swan, *The Forgotten Desert Mothers*, 60.

7. John Chryssavgis, *In the Heart of the Desert: The Spirituality of the Desert Fathers and Mothers* (Bloomington, IN: World Wisdom, 2003), 35.

8. Alan Jones, *Soul Making: The Desert Way of Spirituality* (San Francsico: Harper & Row, 1985), 12.

Chapter 3: The Little World of Ourselves

9. Swan, *The Forgotten Desert Mothers*, 35.

Chaper 4: "Go to Your Cell"

10. Swan, *The Forgotten Desert Mothers*, 47.
11. Benedicta Ward, S.L.G., trans., *The Sayings of the Desert Fathers: The Alphabetical Collection* (Kalamazoo, MI: Cistercian Publications, 1975), 139.

Chapter 5: Learning the Art of Discernment

12. Swan, *The Forgotten Desert Mothers*, 58.
13. See Pseudo-Anthanasius, *The Life and Regimen of the Blessed and Holy Teacher, Syncletica*, trans. Elizabeth Bongie (Toronto: Peregrina, 1995).
14. Parker Palmer, *Let Your Life Speak: Listening for the Voice of Vocation* (San Francisco: Jossey-Bass, 2000).
15. Debra Farrington, *Hearing with the Heart: A Gentle Guide to Discerning God's Will for Your Life* (San Francisco: Jossey-Bass, 2003), 4.
16. The Book of Common Prayer (BCP) (New York: Church Hymnal Corporation, 1979), 101, 125.
17. Chryssavgis, *In the Heart of the Desert*, 45.

Chapter 6: Spiritual Guidance: Lovers of Souls

18. Swan, *The Forgotten Desert Mothers*, 67.
19. Elm, *Virgins of God*, 263.
20. Ibid., 263.
21. Ward, *Sayings of the Desert Fathers*, xxii.
22. Swan, *The Forgotten Desert Mothers*, 52.
23. BCP, 447.
24. BCP, 446.

Chapter 7: The Practice of Humility

25. Swan, *The Forgotten Desert Mothers*, 67.
26. Elm, *Virgins of God*, 264.
27. Bondi, *To Love as God Loves*, 48–49.
28. Ibid., 58.
29. Frederica Mathewes-Green, *The Illumined Heart: The Ancient Christian Path of Transformation* (Brewster, MA: Paraclete, 2001), 48.

30. For a full discussion of each of these passions, please see Bondi, *To Love as God Loves*, 70–77.

31. Chryssavgis, *In the Heart of the Desert*, 53.

32. Ibid., 53.

33. Bondi, *To Love as God Loves*, 43.

Chapter 8: Showing Up Daily, or Becoming an Ascetic

34. Swan, *The Forgotten Desert Mothers*, 54.

35. Bondi, *To Love as God Loves*, 10.

36. Ibid., 22.

37. Chryssavgis, *In the Heart of the Desert*, 30.

Chapter 9: Living a Dedicated Life:
The Ongoing Practice of Listening and Choosing

38. Swan, *The Forgotten Desert Mothers*, 55.

39. Peter Brown, *The Body and Society: Men, Women, and Sexual Renunciation in Early Christianity* (New York: Columbia University Press, 1988), 6.

Chapter 10: Becoming Fully Human

40. Swan, *The Forgotten Desert Mothers*, 40.

41. Chryssavgis, *In the Heart of the Desert*, 40.

42. Hymn 503, v. 1, *Church Hymnal 1982* (New York: Church Hymnal Corporation, 1982).

43. I am grateful to Rev. Jane Patterson for this wording, used in an adult education class at St. Mark's Episcopal Church in San Antonio, Texas, during the fall of 2005.